Golf's Mental Hazards

Overcome Them and Put an End to the Self-Destructive Round

Alan Shapiro, Ph.D.

A FIRESIDE BOOK
PUBLISHED BY SIMON AND SCHUSTER

FIRESIDE
Rockefeller Center
1230 Avenue of the Americas
New York, NY 10020

FIRESIDE and colophon are registered trademarks
of Simon & Schuster Inc.

Designed by Jeffrey L. Ward

Manufactured in the United States of America

10 9 8 7 6

Library of Congress Cataloging-in-Publication Data
Shapiro, Alan.
   Golf's mental hazards : overcome them and put an end to the self-
destructive round / Alan Shapiro.
      p.   cm.
   "A Fireside book."
   Includes bibliographical references (p.   ).
   1. Golf—Psychological aspects.   I. Title.
GV979.P75S53   1996
796.352'01'9—dc20   96-1935
                                                              CIP

ISBN 0-684-80457-3

For my parents,
Anne and William

ACKNOWLEDGMENTS

THE THREE YEARS I HAVE SPENT CONCEPTUALIZING, RESEARCHING, and writing this book have been a joy. How many golfers can step out on the links and honestly state—even while in the throes of a depressingly ugly round—that they are working? There are several individuals I wish to thank for helping me accomplish this grand scam.

Tom DeBerry, head golf professional at Normanside Country Club, got me started with the beginnings of a swing and first suggested that I investigate the mental side of golf. A generous man and astute teacher, Tom quickly recognized that my grasp on human nature and gift of gab probably exceeded my potential for low-handicap golf. I also wish to thank the members of his club who were kind enough to participate in the research portions of this book.

Jay Morelli, Golf Director of the Golf School in Mt. Snow, Vermont, has been inviting me to present my ideas in front of a room full of enrollees several times a season for the past three years. Lecturing at the Golf School seminars helped me sharpen my conceptual focus for this project, so I thank Jay and his staff for their generous hospitality and also the individuals who attended my seminars for their feedback and input.

The transition from golf psychologist to writer was facilitated by a writing course that I attended. The teacher, Pauline Bartel, was instrumental in opening my eyes to the reality of the publishing industry and in shifting the slant of my original book proposal to one that was meaningful to the average golfer. Many thanks to Pauline for her time and expertise.

I am grateful to my agent, Diana Finch, who recognized the value of my book proposal and offered early observations that were critical to the quality of the finished product. I also wish to thank Dan Lane, my editor at Simon & Schuster, who tightened up my tendency toward wordiness, yet permitted enough literary freedom to maintain my desired voice throughout the edited text.

And then there are my golfing buddies who tolerated my steady stream of psychological analysis during play. It was not uncommon for me to refer to the subconscious motive behind a flubbed chip or a crushed drive, to jot down a note or even to tape-record—for anecdotal reference—the details of what I believed to be a cosmic golfing moment. My thanks to Jay Baron, Steve Block, Joe Bullis, Fred Cionek, Dave Cook, Bill Dennis, Lee Eggleston, Tom Fanning, Tom Fitzgerald, Don Frey, Fred Frey, Lester Golderman, Allen Greenberg, Alan Gruber, Steven Javors, Allen Jones, Pete Kukulich, Bob Lahue, Bill Pepe, Jeff Radden, Larry Radden, Kevin Roberts, Larry Rybicki, Neil Schachter, Jeff Schulkind, Bill Schwarz, Don Segal, Adam Shapiro, John Stallmer, Clarke Supley, and Leo Tokryman. Special thanks to Alan, Jeff, and Neil, who rounded out the Myrtle Beach "Core Four," and to the members of the Colonie Golf League.

On the personal front, I wish to thank Jeffrey Radden, a good friend and talented artist, for his generous contribution of time toward the design of the research materials including the test forms used in this book. I owe a large debt of gratitude to my office assistant, Betty Arnold, who made countless phone calls—many of which demanded assertiveness beyond my own capabilities. Betty also handled office emergencies when I was unavailable and fed me a steady stream of bagels to ensure my stamina at the word processor. And finally, my family members are to be thanked. Carrie, Jamie, and Adam remained interested in my writing project and didn't balk about my absence during phases of intensity. My wife, Sandy, offered new meaning to the concept of golf widow. Tolerating my shifts in mood, reading and offering valuable comments on difficult portions of the first draft, she maintained her usual sweet temperament and perhaps even loved me more for my conviction in this project.

CONTENTS

"Golf is the ego and id in a playoff
that never ends. It's a solitary wandering
in the manicured wilderness. It's man alone
with his own mind. It's too much time to
think and too much to think about. It's
more like life than life itself."

—DAVID NOONAN

INTRODUCTION

"Let's face it, 95 percent of this game is mental. A guy plays lousy golf, he doesn't need a pro, he needs a shrink."

—TOM MURPHY

As a clinical psychologist my job is to sit and listen. Hour by hour, I hear the frustrations, problems, hopes, and dreams that people carry with them. I learn about their vulnerabilities, their disappointments, their excitement, and their fears. Hour by hour, day after day, this is my job. And it is a job I love. I have always been fascinated by the workings of the mind and have enjoyed peering past the walls that people build around their private thoughts and inner feelings. Walls designed to protect and keep secret their demons, dreams, and desires. Walls that are intended to prevent others from seeing who they really are.

If I can isolate any single lesson that I have learned from my study of people, it is that none of us are all that unique. Beneath varying facades of personality and the manner in which we present ourselves to others, are fears and self-doubts that are basic components of the human condition. As a self-proclaimed human—complete with my own set of insecurities and vulnerabilities—I have often recognized myself in the faces of those I was treating. And as much as I might love to observe and analyze the mind at work, there comes a point where it is more draining than fascinating, more depressing than uplifting. After

ten years of looking in a mirror each day, I came to recognize the
need for an escape from the daily grind. If I was to avoid burning
out on the job, I had to find something that would refresh and
replenish me, and most notably get me away from the mental
side of life.

I don't know why it took me so long to recognize that golf
might satisfy all of my criteria for the perfect recreational activity.
Several of my oldest and closest friends played golf, but to me it
seemed like such a boring game. I tried to watch it on television,
but all I saw were pastel-shaded mannequins moving around in
slow motion. As much as I wanted to catch the bug, I could not
see myself playing golf. But I was desperate and the more
thought I gave to the subject, the more sense it began to make.
The great game of golf, played in the great outdoors, could possibly be my ticket, thousand of miles away from the dealings of
the mind, from the study of people and their problems. More
and more, I came to believe that this mellow, relaxed game was
just what I needed to give me that second wind as I reached the
turn in my life.

I began in what I thought was a healthy and intelligent manner. A few lessons from a pro, lots of practice with a 7-iron, and
solitary jaunts around lightly traveled par-three courses during
off hours. My expectations at the outset were realistic and mod-
est: "Maybe I'll be ready to play on the big courses next year."
"If I can occasionally break a hundred in five years, I'll be
satisfied."

But then something happened that forever changed my life.
After a few weeks of hacking away at range balls, and banging
around a couple of executive cow pastures, I stepped up to my
ball on the tee of a 142-yard hole and struck a 7-iron crisply, high
and dead straight at the flagstick, the ball settling two feet from
the hole. My tip-in for birdie was a nice finishing touch, but it
was secondary to what that experience did to me. After that
magical moment, golf became more than a simple pursuit of
escapist recreation. It became a frantic and obsessive search for a
reenactment of that moment on the tee, held in my finish, watching the ball in flight. In my mind, I relived that moment over
and over, but could not recall it with the sensory detail that I
knew occurred while I watched the ball in flight. The only an-

swer was to experience it again. And that meant hitting balls. Lots and lots of balls.

The law of averages came around for me, and I experienced my fair share of majestic shots. I don't know why I wasn't frustrated by the scores of toppers and flubs I had to experience in exchange for each perfect hit, but I somehow convinced myself that the good hits were more a reflection of my natural golfing skills and that, with a little practice, I would be hitting them *all* clean and true. I began to secretly play the role of cool hustler, getting ready to knock the socks off my unknowing golfing friends. As a raw beginner, I was already experiencing a fair share of success at this supposedly highly difficult game. I figured that I had some talent, some flair for the game. A little time and effort, and I knew that I could do some serious damage.

The program picked up in intensity. I read Ben Hogan's *Five Lessons: The Modern Fundamentals of Golf*, watched three volumes of Lee Trevino's *Priceless Golf Tips* video series, ran to the driving range during patient cancellations, hit whiffle balls into my neighbor's pool, and broke my dining room fixture while learning how to pick up a ball with the back edge of my putter. Ten weeks after my first lesson, a longtime golf-addict friend of mine from New Jersey called and invited me to join him and a couple of friends at an "open and short" course the following weekend. I felt anxious but ready. A few buckets with my 3-wood and I'd be off the tee, my game complete enough for the test of a real live golf outing on a regulation size course.

I don't remember much about that first round of golf except for a smattering of details and feelings. The first hole was a 525-yard par five with trees on the left and water on the right, both of which I avoided by hitting a 3-wood down the middle . . . about three yards out. I remember turning to the others and seeing a dozen or so men looking away or down, checking their grips, stretching, pretending to have not noticed. I looked to my friend's familiar face for some help, and he responded with: "Go ahead, take out an iron and whack it out there—a nice, easy swing." My legs were weak, my palms moist, and I felt fear and disgrace reminiscent of some of the more forgettable moments of childhood. In my mind I knew I could not hit that golf ball.

I've been hacking away for five years now and I realize I'm

hooked for life. I also realize that I did anything but escape the mental side of life. As a golfer, I am prey to the frustration, anger, anxiety, and passion inherent in the game. I am driven to uncover the magic that will enable me to hit the ball as well as I do in my early-morning dreams, half-awake, hours before tee-time. As a psychologist, I observe myself and I observe other golfers and I ask the question *why*. Why do we experience such an intense range of emotions? Why do some golfers—independent of ability—hold it together in the face of adversity while others self-destruct? Why do golfers spend so much time and money obsessively chasing the goal of impossible mastery?

As a golfer, I've managed to put together a respectable "bo-geyish" game. My progress has entailed hours of lessons and practice designed to understand and better develop a mastery of the fundamentals. I have bought customized golf clubs (my third set in five years) in an effort to minimize flaws in my anatomy and athleticism. And with all the practice, articles read, new swing thoughts, and equipment changes, I cannot get beyond the simple reality that I play this game more with my mind than with my body. I know how it feels to watch shot after shot fly true to the target as I experience the effortless competence that goes with being in "The Zone." I also know what it's like to lose faith in my swing and in myself and stumble into the depths of utter ineptitude.

As a psychologist, my fascination with the way people think and feel has, if anything, been intensified by my introduction to the world of golfers. All recreational goals aside, I have committed myself to better understanding the mental side of this complex and magically seductive game. I have worked with aspiring golf professionals and conducted research on the correlation between personality and golf performance. I have founded *Mental Skills Development,* a seminar company that specializes in the psychology of golf, and I have written this book. Most basic to all that I have learned is the belief that golf is not just a game. Golf is who we are, played in the manner in which we live our lives.

I have learned that both the good and bad personality traits that pervade our daily lives have the capacity to lead to success or failure on the golf course as well as in the workplace or in the home. For instance, the golfer who has first-tee jitters might also be the individual who experiences anxiety in social situations or during interviews. The golfer who responds to a shanked shot by throwing a club is probably the same person who slams doors or kicks walls in response to other moments of frustration.

All in all, I have managed to isolate six traits—"Golf's Mental Hazards"—which, if not attended to, can be particularly obstructive to any hope the golfer may have for game improvement. Those who come to understand and overcome these mental hazards will be in a position to play up to their potential with greater consistency. This book was developed to provide the reader with the tools to accomplish this objective and to finally put an end to the self-destructive round.

What This Book Will Do for You

I REMEMBER A DAY TOWARD THE END OF MY SECOND GOLF SEASON when I was at the practice range, hitting the ball exceptionally well, and I noticed a teaching pro giving a man who was approximately my age a lesson. Even though I was feeling pretty good about my game at the moment, there's nothing better for the ego than to watch a fellow golfer suffer. I inched a little closer and listened to their discussion.

"I don't know how I can play in that tournament tomorrow," said the exasperated student, who was topping the ball, off to the right. "It's going to be a nightmare. Maybe I should just cancel and take more time to practice."

"You're not that far off the mark," offered the pro. "Your swing's not half bad. You're just stopping on the downswing. Your hands aren't getting through, which is leaving the clubface open at impact."

"Okay, let me try again," replied the student.

Same result.

If the pro was frustrated, he didn't show it. The student looked to be on the verge of tears.

"I want you to try something for me," suggested the pro. "Take out your nine-iron and take a few half swings. As if you were chipping."

The student complied.

"Now hit one off the tee. A nice and easy, rhythmic swing. And make sure you keep your head behind the ball. Don't even look up after you've made contact."

The student hit the ball high and straight, just short of the 100-yard marker and repeated the process successfully for several more shots. Gradually, the pro lengthened his student's swing and worked him up to his 3-wood. The results were amazing. The guy couldn't miss. In fact, my own ego was quick to deflate when I came to realize that when on his game, this fellow hit the ball with more authority than I did. He was flying high and I was feeling down. Before leaving, I made sure to stop at the pro shop and take note of the teacher's name.

There's little doubt that the effective golf pro must also be a good psychologist. It's not difficult to find an instructor who knows the fundamentals of the golf swing, but how about one who can read people and inject them with confidence? A good pro knows that not all instructional approaches will be successful with all students. In addition to evaluating swing plane, weight shift, and clubhead speed, the successful golf instructor makes a study of the student's expectations and temperament. A master of reading people's individual styles and sets of needs, the master teacher then goes about the business of administering a customized plan for improvement.

Psychologists approach people in much the same manner. Realizing that not all approaches will work successfully for all types of individuals, the psychologist first conducts an evaluation. This step involves observation and clinical interview and oftentimes includes the administration of personality tests. This being a book about the psychology of golf, it seems fitting that the approach taken should follow the same individualized format that is practiced by effective golf instructors and psychologists. To help accomplish this objective, I have developed the *Mental Hazard Assessment Scale (MHAS)*.

The *MHAS* is a test that is designed to help you develop your Mental Hazard Profile, or an individualized account of your qualities of temperament that result in the self-destructive round. To determine the extent to which each of Golf's Mental Hazards impacts on your golf performance, you will self-administer and score the 48-question *MHAS* which can be found in Chapter 2. The following is a brief description of each of Golf's Mental Hazards:

- **HAZARD ONE—The Fear of Fear**
  Applies to golfers who are fearful, apprehensive, with a tendency to worry. Golfers who fall prey to this hazard experience anticipatory anxiety before a round, have first-tee jitters, and tend to "choke" during critical moments of a match.
- **HAZARD TWO—Losing Your Cool**
  This golfer does not tolerate frustration very well; such players will readily lose their cool when things don't go their way. This is the golfer who slams the club into the ground, throws it into a water hazard, or wraps it around a tree.
- **HAZARD THREE—Getting Too Up or Too Down**
  Golfers vulnerable to Hazard Three are easily discouraged and quick to get down on themselves. Their emotions can range from euphoria after making a difficult par to utter despair after knocking a tee shot out-of-bounds on the very next hole. On the basis of performance on any given day, these golfers can remain elated or depressed for hours or even days after a round of golf.
- **HAZARD FOUR—Worrying What Others Think**
  Golfers who experience difficulty with the fourth hazard are generally self-conscious individuals who dread embarrassment on the golf course. These individuals are prone to feelings of inferiority, are sensitive to ridicule, and typically feel like others are watching and judging.
- **HAZARD FIVE—The Need to Be in Control**
  This golfer is an overly analytical thinker who experiences difficulty with the intuitive, more feel-oriented part of the game. This "control-freak" golfer has problems with self-trust and will frequently freeze up before beginning the swing.
- **HAZARD SIX—An Unwillingness To Work**
  Golf might be a relaxing game that requires little effort for some, but good steady play requires bear-down effort and periods of intense concentration. Golfers who struggle with Hazard Six are easily bored. They want results, but are not

willing to put in the time or effort to work toward accomplishing goals. This type of golfer is generally lackadaisical,
tending to practice the parts of the game that he or she most
enjoys or has the least difficulty with.

After completing the *MHAS*, you will possess your own Mental Hazard Profile telling you which of the six hazards is most
likely leading to your self-destructive round. Each hazard has
been given its own chapter, complete with common symptoms
and techniques for overcoming them. The remaining chapters
cover an assortment of topics that pertain to the psychology of
golf performance.

1

A Matter of Life and Death?

 "Like life, golf can be humbling. However, little good comes from brooding about mistakes we've made. The next shot, in golf or in life, is the big one."

—GRANTLAND RICE

I RECALL A CONVERSATION WITH A MIDDLE-AGED ACQUAINTANCE who loved to participate in sports but found that his basketball and softball days were pretty much finished. All of my attempts at selling him on golf were futile. "Too boring" or "It's not a real sport" was his objection. I kept pushing until the truth finally came out. "I'm not going to get into golf until I can really get into it. Probably not until I retire. You golfers are crazy. It's all you eat, sleep, and breathe. Golf's not a game. It's insanity. No, golf's not a game. Golf's . . . golf's . . . life!"

This reluctant golfer was onto something. As obsessions, compulsions, addictions, and all fanatical pursuits go, golf is probably one of the more harmless of life-altering activities. But still, golf has a special power over its followers. And not unlike most powerful influences, it can have a negative impact or it can yield positive, life-enhancing outcomes.

Are You Your Golf Game?

IN THE NEXT CHAPTER, YOU WILL HAVE THE OPPORTUNITY TO SELF-administer the *Mental Hazard Assessment Scale (MHAS)*. But before you take this test and consider the information that it will provide, take an honest look at yourself. What kind of person are you? Are you a nervous, worrier type? Does your temper get the best of you sometimes? Do your moods affect the people around you? Do you worry about the way other people see you? Do you try to control the lives of others? Do you see yourself as a lazy, chronic underachiever?

Next, consider whether these attributes are evident in your golf game. Do you enjoy your time on the golf course, find it relaxing and peaceful? If you answered affirmatively, golf is clearly playing a positive role in your life. On the other hand, if your response was more along the lines of maybe, sometimes, or it depends, the answer is less clear, and some honest self-examination is probably in order.

Nobody is perfect. Everyone has, to some extent, some form of a dark side that acts out in anger, fear, or jealousy. And because golf is played with the same whole body and mind that lives the rest of your life, these qualities, to some extent, will carry over to your golf game. It is important, however, to be aware that this has both positive and negative implications. On the plus side, while you are eliminating hazardous, self-destructive tendencies on the golf course, you can work on qualities of temperament that impede your everyday life. You can become a better golfer and a better person as part of the same process.

Conversely, due to the impossible nature of the game, your golf performance will oftentimes be disappointing, setting you up for frustration and despair. Keep in mind, and remind yourself again and again, that hitting a green or sinking a birdie putt is not the sole determinant of your self-worth. It will not be what determines whether or not your kids go to college. And even if it did, your life would still encompass a broader base than that which is measured by golf performance. This is true even for golfers who depend on golf success for their livelihood. Successful pros are quick to rank their game in order of importance behind a relationship with God and their families. They recognize that even though their livelihood is dependent on golf performance, it is still not a matter of life and death.

Do You Cheat?

I RECALL STANDING IN FRONT OF AN AUDIENCE OF GOLF SCHOOL enrollees and proclaiming that "I have cheated at golf." The audience remained silent while I paused before adding that "Of course, I did so with good reason" and the tension was broken by nervous laughter.

With the exception of PGA professionals playing under the watchful scrutiny of marshals and television cameras, virtually everyone cheats at golf. When you record an 88 on the scorecard, did you take the necessary penalties for moving "unmovable" branches or for rolling your ball out of a divot? Did you accept a not necessarily makable gimme putt? In his *Little Red Book,* the late Harvey Penick expressed with certainty that the average American golfer, if every stroke was recorded in observance of strict USGA guidelines, seldom broke 100.

Because golf performance so readily becomes tied to feelings of overall self-worth, the game brings out the fraud in people more than most other games. The golfer's score impacts on handicap, and handicap becomes a defining quality of identity. ("I'm a 15." "Oh really? I'm a 4.") As a result, there is a potentially face-saving, status-building motive to cheat and keep scores down.

And it is not about money. No, golfers seldom cheat to win a buck. It's more about ego and the pursuit of a lower score and a lower handicap. It has been my observation that the practice of "sandbagging"—or the inflating of handicap to earn low net victories—is far less common than the fraud enacted for the purpose of being represented as a "better" golfer with a lower handicap. I know that when I watch televised Pro-Ams and see an amateur with a 13 handicap and a swing that's uglier than the typical weekend hacker, something is very much wrong. For most, a lower handicap with the always plausible excuse of a simply "bad day" is more desirable than the honest admission of being a consistently poor golfer.

The question is not whether you cheat. The question is what *kind* of cheater you are, and how much into denial you are about your fraudulent ways. Is your manner of cheating generally practiced and accepted by your playing partners or is it secretive and deceptive? Again, because golf imitates life, consider the fraud that comprises the rest of your life. Do you cheat at cards, on your income tax, on your spouse? Do you lie a lot or a little, exaggerating details to make yourself appear wealthier, smarter, or more athletic? If you do, welcome to the club. None of us are so godly as to be entirely self-assured and comfortable with who we are.

Keep in mind that all unhealthy behaviors come down to the degree to which they are practiced as well as to the degree to which they are recognized. The next time you "Florsheim" one out from behind a tree, forget the second one out of the trap, or suffer a mathematical brain cramp that does not permit counting any higher than six, know what you're doing and be honest with yourself about it. It's trite just to remind you that "you're only cheating yourself," so I will remind you of two further points that make the practice of cheating a highly impractical activity. For one, nobody cares or for that matter judges you on the basis of your handicap. If you're a nice person who is fun to be around, you'll be respected and appreciated. The second point for you sneaky cheats is that you are not fooling anybody. Everyone knows who you are. Which means that you have not only failed to gain the admiration of playing partners, but very likely lost their respect, along with a tad of self-respect as part of the bargain.

Are Golfers Masochists?

HAVING MADE AND ACCEPTED MY VOWS TO THE GAME OF GOLF, MY next question is why. I guess I can also ask why I took my marriage vows some twenty-three years ago. Golf is not that unlike a marriage. Good times, bad times, love, hate, hard work. And I guess that there is something to be said about commitment. Marriage makes sense for me but golf is another story.

Do you torture yourself by playing a lot of golf even while slumping or continue to have high expectations after a string of horrible rounds? Have you ever noticed that even when golf is not much fun—when all the members of your group are mumbling, withdrawn, cranky—it somehow gets re-created in a favorable light after the fact? Having fallen prey to all of these situations, I can't help but wonder if I might not be some kind of masochist.

It is a simple fact of life that sometimes actual experiences just can't compete with our anticipation of them. It's also true that there is a tendency to reconstruct memories of events after they occur in a manner that filters out the bad feelings. Consider the family that decides to visit Disneyworld for a second time. Memories of the first vacation effectively omit the sibling angst, the spousal angst, the heat, the lines, the $3.00 Cokes, the ten-hour layover at the airport. Pleasant and seemingly joyous photos and videos do not reveal any of these nightmarish details. What *is* apparent are the handful of joyous moments along with the excitement of anticipation that preceded the trip.

Golfers are not any more masochistic than anyone else. They are just employing the same rules for processing "reality" that apply to all life situations. Remember those rounds when you struggled until suddenly hitting a pitch shot from sixty yards out to ten inches from the stick or really nailing a drive. Someone was certain to state, "That's the one you'll remember" or "That'll keep you comin' back." And it's true. Not unlike electroconvulsive shock treatments, the occasional great moment injects you with a surge that wipes out selective portions of your memory. What will constitute subsequent states of anticipation will be those great moments—a couple of greens in regulation, a crushed drive down the middle, an impossible, scrambling par —when all was well in your mind and spirit.

When Does It Become Unhealthy?

SEVERAL YEARS BACK, BEFORE I BEGAN TO PLAY GOLF, I HAD A woman patient who came to see me for the purpose of discussing her decision to leave her husband. Cindi's reason, as she explained it, was that she had had enough of life as a golf widow. She explained to me that alcohol almost ended their marriage several years back. At that time, Cindi also was prepared to leave, which prompted the beginning of Bob's sobriety. The current problem was Bob's obsession with golf. During the six-month season, he played in two evening leagues and on both weekend mornings. On the evenings he didn't play, he would go to the driving range. When home, he read golf magazines, watched golf videos, and practiced putting on the living-room carpet. Saturday and Sunday afternoons were spent watching golf on television. When he played well, Bob was upbeat and talkative. When he had a disappointing round, everyone knew to give him his space. During the winter months, he worked, ate, watched television, and slept. He didn't show much sign of life until March, when a local heated range opened up, and he began preparing for the next season.

After a couple of individual sessions with Cindi, I had an opportunity to meet Bob, who openly and I believe honestly presented his side of the situation.

> *I gave up drinking because I came to realize that I was hurting my family. I've been sober for five years now and my recovery is the most important thing in my life. Sure I play a lot of golf, but is that so bad? Did Cindi tell you that I also go to AA meetings at least once and sometimes twice a week? And did she tell you how devoted I am to our kids? I never miss a school function, dance recital, or Little League game. I know the golf gets to her, but Jesus, I'm doing the best I can do. Would she rather me be at the bars or out on the golf course?*

Bob made an interesting case for himself. Nobody's perfect and he was a good provider and a loving father. Given the range of pathological behavior I observe in my practice, golf nut did not seem all that bad. It was not until I began seeing Bob and Cindi as a couple that I came to realize that Bob was not lying to Cindi or to me. Bob was lying to himself. It was not the hours that Bob put into his golf game that were the problem. It was the fact that he was depressed and was using the golf obsession as a way to mask this depression. In much the same manner that he used alcohol, Bob used golf to avoid the feelings and interpersonal intimacy that he needed for a well-adjusted life. In current-day psychological jargon, Bob had stopped drinking, but had switched compulsions, had found a substitute addiction. Bob was a dry drunk.

During the three months of counseling that followed, Cindi stuck to her guns regarding her threat to leave. Bob subsequently found a new AA sponsor (his previous one had a 3 handicap) and reexamined the work he had done on the Twelve Steps of Alcoholics Anonymous. Although he did not substantially cut back the hours he put into playing and practicing, Bob did restructure his perception of the role that golf played in his life. The most notable change, from Bob's point of view, was that he enjoyed playing more than he had in years, and was free of the depression and guilt that were part and parcel of the isolated, never satisfied existence that he left behind.

Bob's case study is a rather extreme example of golf becoming an unhealthy obsession. This is clearly not the case for more casual golfers who see the game as an opportunity for escape from the routine and for an occasional moment of glory. But there are those golfers who, although not as fanatical as Bob, still take their game a bit too seriously.

As was the case with Bob, golf has the potential to be a mood-altering, addictive activity that can enable the avoidance of dealing with *real* problems. You can tell if you're ready for Golfers' Anonymous by asking yourself the following questions: What is the state of my personal relationships? Would others who are close to me agree with this assessment? Is my work gratifying, and do I get along well with co-workers? So long as you remain honest with yourself and keep your priorities straight, go ahead and indulge yourself in the wonderful escape that golf provides. As escapes go, golf is a reasonably healthy choice. Just remember that golf is not what your life is about, but rather is a *game* that *simulates* real life. In and out of hazards, the joy and despair of it all, golf is the ultimate experience in virtual, but not actual reality.

The Opportunity That Golf Provides

NOT ALL GOLFERS ARE INTERESTED IN OR NEED THE TYPE OF IN-depth analysis I have suggested in the previous section. But I'd bet the house and kids on the prediction that almost all golfers would do whatever they could to knock a few strokes off their handicap. If your nerves, anger, or mood swings are impeding your ability to play up to your potential, you have got to learn how to control these behaviors if you stand any chance of improving your game. The problem, as I've already stated it, is that the person cannot be separated from the golfer. If you're moody and irritable at home or on the job, you're going to react similarly when things don't go as planned on the golf course.

Golf provides the perfect opportunity to explore your inner feelings of self-worth, self-acceptance, and peace of mind. In effect, this journey into self represents the primary objective of the remaining portions of this book. The first step in the process takes place in the following chapter with the administration of the *Mental Hazard Assessment Scale*. This questionnaire will help you to gain insight into the mental hazards that govern your daily life as well as your golf game. If you're the type who is not particularly comfortable with self-analysis, take the test anyway. If you don't feel the need for personal growth, do it for the spouse, kids, friends, co-workers, and dog. And do it to fuel the dream of a steady, relaxed, repeating swing. And for the look on your partner's face when he's finally the one reaching for his wallet at the 19th hole!

2

Your Mental Hazard Profile

"A moment's insight is sometimes worth a life's experience."

—OLIVER WENDELL HOLMES, SR.

THE FIRST STEP IN ANY CHANGE PROCESS IS KNOWING WHAT IT IS that needs to be changed. This chapter will give you the opportunity to self-administer the *Mental Hazard Assessment Scale (MHAS)* in order to accomplish this objective. After taking the 48-item test, you will be given instructions for scoring it and for interpreting the scores within the context of your Mental Hazard Profile. At the completion of this chapter, you will know which of Golf's Mental Hazards give you little trouble, as well as which are responsible for the self-destructive golf round. In a broader sense, you will gain insight into the "hazardous" qualities of your temperament that give you the most difficulty in the course of your daily life.

Administration of the MHAS

FOLLOW THE INSTRUCTIONS FOR THE SELF-ADMINISTRATION OF the *MHAS*. Do not take a great deal of time struggling to determine the absolutely *correct* response for any of the items. Rather, go through the test quickly, recording the responses that first occur to you. If it has taken more than a minute or so to determine whether an item is true or false, and you still find yourself unsure, select the *neutral* response item.

MENTAL HAZARD ASSESSMENT SCALE

Respond to each of the following statements by filling in the space to the left with either a **T**, **F**, or **N**. Go through the items quickly, entering the response that first occurs to you.

FILL IN:
T if you believe the statement is true most of the time.
F if you believe the statement is false most of the time.
N if you cannot determine whether the statement is true or false.

___ 1. I am not the type of person who worries about many things.

___ 2. It doesn't take much to tick me off.

___ 3. It's not my style to get depressed or down for very long.

___ 4. While engaged in conversation, I worry about saying something that will embarrass me.

___ 5. I enjoy activities that are planned as opposed to doing things spontaneously.

___ 6. I'd be a much better golfer if I enjoyed practicing more.

___ 7. When I am having an especially good round, I don't expect it to last.

___ 8. After blowing an easy scoring opportunity, I compose myself pretty quickly.

___ 9. I get down on myself very easily and very often.

___ 10. When I have a poor round of golf, I feel embarrassed and ashamed.

___ 11. I am sometimes described by friends as being free-spirited.

___ 12. When I have many small tasks to do, I sometimes do nothing at all.

___ 13. It is not unusual for me to feel physical signs of nervousness.

___ 14. I often feel like throwing my club.

___ 15. When in a slump, I feel like giving up the game altogether.

___ 16. I seldom worry about how others see me.

___ 17. I tend to overanalyze my golf swing.

___ 18. I see myself as having perfectionist qualities.

___ 19. It is extremely rare for me to have problems sleeping the night before a golf outing.

___ 20. I have often been described as having a short fuse.

___ 21. I am usually upbeat and cheerful.

___ 22. It matters to me that others are impressed with my game.

___ 23. I have more faith in logical conclusions than in intuition.

___ 24. I don't spend much time working on the weak areas of my game.

___ 25. Close friends have told me that I'm a "worry-wart."

___ 26. I have little patience when play gets slow.

___ 27. A bad round of golf can ruin my entire day.

___ 28. I feel embarrassed when someone else behaves in a foolish manner.

___ 29. I tend to "freeze up" when I stand over my ball.

___ 30. I have little patience for going through a routine before every shot.

___ 31. Waiting on the first tee, I often feel physical signs of anxiety.

___ 32. I see myself as patient and tolerant.

___ 33. If I'm going to blame anyone for a mishap, it'll probably be myself.

___ 34. It's hard for me to feel good about my game when I play with better golfers.

___ 35. I'm a player who relies more on feel than on mechanics.

___ 36. It's extremely unusual for me to miss a day of work.

___ 37. I am definitely uptight too much of the time.

___ 38. Some golfers are so inept, they have no right being allowed on a golf course.

___ 39. When I'm playing poorly, a sinking, almost sick feeling comes over me.

___ 40. Before an important round, I worry about getting off the first tee in a decent fashion.

___ 41. It is better to rely on thoughts than on feelings.

___ 42. When I'm having a poor round, I tend to rush up to my ball and just whack it.

___ 43. It usually takes me a few holes before I settle down and play decent golf.

I 44. If someone cuts me off in traffic, I want to get back at that person.

I 45. I am dissatisfied with many parts of my game.

I 46. I am seldom intimidated by other people.

F 47. I carefully consider all my options before taking a shot.

T 48. I'm quick out of the gate, but often have trouble following through on projects.

Now transfer your answers to the response sheet.

The response sheet is located on the following page. Take note of the way items are numbered, making sure to enter your responses across the page rather than down each column. On top of each column, you will see the letters, T, N, and F. Make sure that you check the box that corresponds to the response that you have placed in the space to the left of each of the above items. Ignore the numbers located inside of the boxes you will be checking. They will be used for scoring the scale after you have completed transferring your responses.

MENTAL HAZARD ASSESSMENT SCALE
RESPONSE SHEET

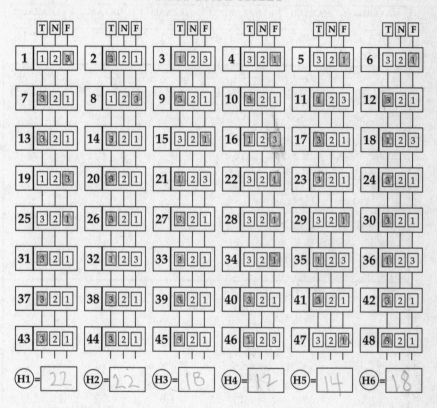

(H1)= 22   (H2)= 22   (H3)= 18   (H4)= 12   (H5)= 14   (H6)= 18

Calculate Your Scores

For each of the six columns, add up the eight numbers that are in the boxes that you have checked. Enter six totals in the boxes labeled H1 through H6. Your scores will range from eight to twenty-four.

Transfer Your Score to Your Mental Hazard Profile

Take each of the six scores for H1-H6 and enter them in the appropriate squares which are located across the top of the Mental Hazard Profile, found on the following page. Circle the number in the column which runs down from each of the six scores.

MENTAL HAZARD PROFILE

HAZARD ONE	HAZARD TWO	HAZARD THREE	HAZARD FOUR	HAZARD FIVE	HAZARD SIX
22	*22*	*18*	*12*	*14*	*18*

ELEVATED RANGE

HAZARD ONE	HAZARD TWO	HAZARD THREE	HAZARD FOUR	HAZARD FIVE	HAZARD SIX
21-24	21-24	20-24	21-24	22-24	22-24
20	20	19	20	21	21
19	19	18	19	20	20
18	18	17	18	19	19
17	17	16	17	18	18
16	16	15	16	17	17

MODERATE RANGE

15	15	14	15	16	16
14	14	13	14	15	15
13	13	12	13	14	14
12	12	11	12	13	13

LOW RANGE

11	11	10	11	12	12
-	-	-	-	11	11
10	10	9	10	10	10
9	9	-	9	9	9
8	8	8	8	8	8

Interpreting Your Mental Hazard Profile

Look at the pattern of your scores on the Mental Hazard Profile. Mental hazard scores that fall in the elevated range of the table indicate problem areas. Scores falling in the low range of the table represent areas that are not particularly troublesome. Mental hazard scores in the moderate range indicate that you experience as much difficulty with the mental hazard in question as did the average person who took this test as part of the research sample. The data generated by this sample are summarized in the Appendix, at the back of this book.

Although the range of scores on the Mental Hazard Profile is designated as either elevated, moderate, or low, it is important to understand that this range is actually a continuous scale, not simply broken into three separate and independent parts. For this reason, make sure to consider whether the scores fall in the upper or the lower portion of their designated range. For instance, a score of 15 as opposed to 12 for Hazard One should not be interpreted as simply falling into the moderate range. Likewise, a score of 22 and one of 15 for Hazard Three, although both are located in the elevated range, have very different meanings.

The MHAS and Personality

Personality refers to a set of stable traits that people predictably display over the course of their lives. Some people are worriers, others more laid-back. Some are quiet and withdrawn, others gregarious and extroverted. Some are open to new experiences and impulsive, others need to reflect on matters and tend to resist any kind of novel activity. Personality tests measure these long-term behavioral tendencies.

Even though the *MHAS* bears a good many similarities to these types of test instruments, it is *not* designed to serve the function that a comprehensive personality test accomplishes. Although the type of questions might be similar to those found on personality tests, the *MHAS* examines only those personality qualities that I have observed during the course of my experience as being tied into golf performance. For example, one personality trait that *is not* measured by the *MHAS* is the degree to which an individual is introverted or extroverted. One need not look beyond a comparison of the styles of Ben Hogan and Lee Trevino to be convinced that golf can be played successfully by either a quiet and withdrawn person or one who is gregarious and outgoing.

Can the Golfer Be Separated from the Person?

IT IS A BASIC PREMISE OF THIS BOOK THAT PEOPLE PLAY GOLF IN A manner not unlike the way they live their lives. When you took the *MHAS*, you probably noticed that half of the questions specifically pertained to golf and the other half to nongolf matters. It is therefore possible to score in the elevated range for one of the hazards on the basis of questions that apply exclusively to golf or relate only to nongolf characteristics. After reviewing the data, I have learned that although this is possible, it is unlikely. By analyzing the golf half against the nongolf half of the test, I have determined that approximately 87 percent of the research sample who registered scores in the elevated range for any of the six hazards reported experiencing difficulty with the hazard both on and off the golf course. Even if you are in the 13 percent who might, for instance, experience anxiety, anger, or mood swings on the golf course but not in your everyday life (or vice versa), you will still benefit from a careful probe of the chapter which details the elevated scores on your Mental Hazard Profile.

How to Proceed with This Book

THE NEXT SIX CHAPTERS DETAIL TECHNIQUES AND IDEOLOGIES FOR overcoming each of the six mental hazards. Even if you discover that you are high on three of the hazards and low on the other three, you will still derive benefit by reading all six of the hazard chapters. Your Mental Hazard Profile will inform you of which hazards are elevated as compared with most of the people in the research sample. This does not mean that the hazard in question presents you with *zero* difficulty. For instance, a low score for Hazard One does not necessarily mean that you never experience any problems with anxiety. It simply means that you have less of a problem with it than might be regarded as average.

Particular attention should be paid to those chapters that pertain to the hazards for which you recorded scores in the elevated range. Mental hazard scores in the moderate range, particularly in the upper half of this range, indicate that the information provided in the corresponding chapter will also prove to be very helpful.

Golf's Mental Hazards can be worked at and improved upon. After you have read this book and taken a few months to employ the suggestions for overcoming the various mental hazards, self-administer the *Mental Hazard Assessment Scale* a second time and compare the results with your current scores. At the end of the book you will find a second blank *MHAS* Response Sheet and Mental Hazard Profile form to allow you the opportunity to self-administer this retest.

3

HAZARD ONE:
The Fear of Fear

"I saw that all the things I feared and which
feared me had nothing good or bad in
them save in so far as the mind was
affected by them."

—SPINOZA

*Arnie's alarm was set for 6:20 A.M., but he had been awake since
4:18. Today was the first day of his club's championship matches. He
had taken lessons and put in long hours of practice to get his handicap down to 15. With improved weight shift and balance—no longer
falling back on his heels—the golf swing had become much simpler
for Arnie to execute. No swing thoughts, no worrying about mechanics, just take the club back slowly and come through the ball with a
nice, easy rhythm. Just relax and play your game, thinks Arnie, and
the third-flight championship could be yours.*

*Driving to the course, Arnie plays out the first hole in his mind's
eye. A 3-wood down the center of the fairway, a straight-ahead 7-iron
to the green. No sweat to get up and down for birdie. Despite his
bogey game, Arnie can't imagine not making par on every hole. He
takes a deep breath as he pulls into his club's parking lot and spots
the men beginning to gather around the first tee.*

*All goes well for Arnie at the practice range, from majestically
struck, high-flying 7-irons to his final practice shot—a booming
3-wood that flies directly over the 200-yard marker. A dozen or so
balls remain in his bucket, but he knows he is ready. Arnie wants to
take that last shot with him to the first tee.*

His foursome is next to hit. Arnie stays loose by stretching and taking a few practice swings. "Whoooosh!" A ball explodes off the clubface of the guy on the tee. Must have traveled 260. Arnie continues his routine of taking easy and fluid practice swings until suddenly noticing subtle changes in the way his body feels. There is a wobbly weakness in his legs and his upper body begins to feel tight. He notices a gnawing, buzzing queasiness in his stomach. Arnie just wants to get up there and hit. Head up the damn fairway, into the quiet, more solitary depths of the forested golf course. Away from all this first-tee hoopla.

Arnie's foursome is up. Here it is, he thinks as he watches the first of his group pull it low and left into the base of a pine tree. Walking toward the tee, his turn to hit, Arnie locks gazes with the man who just found trouble and recognizes the face of fear. And then he hears its voice. "It's so important that you play well today. You know how easy it is to mess up when the pressure's on." For Arnie, this is a familiar message from the "devil"—that master saboteur who resides and waits somewhere beneath the surface of conscious awareness. Again Arnie feels his stomach turn and his knees weaken. He tries his best to pretend that he didn't hear that voice. Stepping up to the first-tee in a match that means so much to him, he tries his best to regain the positive, self-confident mind-set that was his just moments earlier. But it is too late, for once the devil pays a visit, the reassuring voice of calm reason is nowhere to be found.

Do you understand what Arnie was experiencing? Do you think he came around and played well that day? Would you know how to handle a similar situation? If you've been playing the game for a while, if you've been alive for a while, you have experienced battles with anxiety or fear both on and off the golf course. All golfers, ranging from high-handicappers to professionals, face the Hazard One challenge all the time. It is given treatment as the first of Golf's Mental Hazards because anxiety is the most insidious and pervasive cause of the self-destructive round. Even if you obtained a low score on the *MHAS* for Hazard One, you no doubt recognize and at some point have done battle with the voice of self-doubt that was represented by Arnie's "devil."

Hazard One Characteristics

ALTHOUGH IT IS A FACT THAT EVERYONE EXPERIENCES ANXIETY, not everyone experiences it to the same degree. Genetically determined personality traits as well as variations in life experience can render some individuals more predisposed to the experience of anxiety than others. Those of you with high scores for Hazard One are not successfully managing this emotion, in part because you just naturally experience *more* anxiety than the average person. You are more sensitive, reactive, analytical, and aware of bodily sensations than most people. These special qualities are both a blessing and a curse. On the positive side, you have a rich emotional life and you can empathize with the feelings of others. On the downside are those moments when you cannot retract your antennae. Hyperaware and supersensitive, not much escapes your attention.

As a Hazard One golfer, your plight is a function of both your body *and* your mind. On the bodily side, you are very sensitive to your physiology. If your heart skips a beat or your stomach flutters for an instant, you are aware of these anatomical subtleties. Mild increases in arousal, which produce even small increments of increased adrenaline output, do not escape your attention. More than many individuals, you very quickly notice the tingling in your arms and legs, the increase in heart rate, the dryness in your mouth that results from this aroused state. But most critical to your tendency to be victimized by anxiety is the manner in which you react to these bodily sensations.

The mind of the Hazard One golfer seldom takes a break. You are analytical types who are always thinking, oftentimes worrying, seeking to understand everything. It is your thought process, the manner in which you cognitively respond to or interpret what your body experiences, that can potentially escalate base levels of anxiety into full-scale panic. If there is a subtle change in your physiology, not only are you quick to notice it, you also need to know *why* it is happening and what is causing it. If the answer cannot be immediately attributed to an apparent experience, you tend to react fearfully. In turn, this fearful reaction further intensifies the physical sensation. This cycle of reacting and counterreacting creates a "snowballing" effect which eventually leads to a disabling level of anxiety and a self-destructive round of golf.

All golfers might have to deal with fear, but Hazard One golfers also have to deal with the fear of fear. That is, with anticipatory anxiety or the fear that you *will* be afraid and not perform up to your potential when the moment of truth finally arrives. Let's go back to Arnie, the case study that opened this chapter. Countless times when Arnie experienced a normal case of nerves he failed to understand what he was experiencing, and he reacted fearfully, which resulted in the proverbial "choke." With these self-destructive experiences etched in Arnie's memory, the fear of fear had become a well-ingrained, deeply programmed habit. The moment Arnie's knees weakened, his mind knew exactly where it all was heading.

If you struggle with Hazard One, your own history of self-destructive anxiety, when coupled with your tendency to worry, leaves you wondering and worrying when the next choke might occur. Even while in the middle of a good round, you might suddenly "wake up" and remember that it might not last. That you have the potential to lose it and play ugly. And needless to say, your worst nightmares can sometimes come true. The first missed putt, flubbed drive, or fat iron shot is all the reminder you need. The Hazard One golfer doesn't even have to be *in* the actual golfing situation to have his or her game impeded by the fear of fear. Upon awakening, driving to the course, or checking in with the starter, the voice of self-doubt might appear. You must come to understand that you are being attacked not by *the* devil, but rather by a devilish and powerful force that is based in your sensitivity and thoughts. A force that can be traced to your inability to understand and handle anxiety.

The Nature of Anxiety

ANXIETY IS A NORMAL AND NECESSARY EMOTION. IT IS BASED ON a genetically evolved "fight-or-flight" reaction that at one time was necessary to save man from "the jaws of the beast." If a caveman was being charged by a wild animal, his autonomic nervous system switched on, resulting in a host of physical changes that included accelerated heartbeat, increased sweating, faster breathing, and muscle tension. These physiological changes equipped the caveman with the skills necessary for survival.

The increase in heartrate permitted blood to be pumped to the larger muscle groups of the outer extremities. Increased perspiration allowed the body to remain cool enough to continue burning off energy, and faster breathing got more oxygen into the bloodstream. Muscle tension allowed sudden or powerful moves to occur in immediate response to attack. The caveman was ready to do whatever it took to survive—to either hang in and fight or get the hell out of there.

Hazard One golfers—complete with a turbo-charged survival instinct—can potentially make a "life-and-death" matter over any worrisome issue. Your autonomic nervous systems do not "see" what is actually being experienced and might not distinguish a charging animal from a par putt, money worries, or a boss with a woeful expression on his face. All you know is that you are being threatened, and if the mind and body engage in their snowballing exchange, your gut reacts as if you are about to die. The nineteenth-century philosopher-psychologist William James knew this when he characterized the basic death anxiety as "the worm at the core" of all fearful reactions.

So there you have it. The reason you "yipped" what should have been that gimme par putt or sliced that critical tee shot on 18 into the woods was that you were afraid you were going to die. Dramatically overstated? Perhaps. Let's suffice it to say that, at the very least, golf has the potential to be a very frightening sport and that the reason you blew that critical shot was that you cared so deeply about pulling it off successfully. As a Hazard One golfer, when you care about something, you care about it intensely. And this intensity can very easily run counter to the relaxed mind and body that are so critical to a rhythmic and productive golf swing.

Harnessing Your Fear

THOSE OF YOU WHO ENGAGE IN REGULAR BATTLE WITH HAZARD One have no doubt experienced your moments of glory. Those instances where you performed well *despite* feeling afraid. The power of fear as a destructive force is easy to recognize and understand. Less obvious is the manner in which this same force can be harnessed and channeled in a positive manner. Feeling fear means you care and are motivated to do whatever it takes to be successful. Consider the alternative. Experiencing no anxiety is an unmotivated, bored, lackadaisical state that provides very little performance energy.

It is for this reason that so many athletes welcome anxiety. Tom Kite stated that "It is a very positive event, being nervous. It allows you to do great things." Think of those moments when you willed a 40-yard pitch shot right at the stick, or you mustered up the power supply to add an extra 20 yards onto a drive. Do you remember the empowered calm you felt, the undeniable belief that you would do what you needed to do? You might not have realized it, but during these instances, you were very likely scared out of your bird. The difference between these moments and other fearful instances where you did not perform well was the way you managed the situation. During peak performances, the surplus adrenaline acted as an efficient fuel, energizing your body and sharpening your senses. When in choke mode, you failed to recognize the positive force of your emotional and physical state. You became afraid of the feelings, afraid of the potential for disaster. By failing to understand the fear of fear, you were again victimized by the devil that is yourself.

Understanding how and why you react to anxiety might be important, but in and of itself, insight does not make the problem go away. The remaining portions of this chapter are designed to supplement insight with technique. You will learn methods designed to reduce the physiological reactions of autonomic activity. Then you will develop the ability to restructure your thinking patterns. You will learn how to reinterpret bodily sensations and alter the negative thoughts that occur automatically during pressure moments. Finally, behavioral routines designed to help you maintain your newfound control over problems with anxiety will be suggested.

The Importance of Proper Breathing

THINK OF WHAT USUALLY HAPPENS TO YOUR GOLF SWING WHEN you are nervous. If you're like most golfers, your swing becomes quicker, disrupting any chance for good rhythm. As a result of a hurried backswing, you may fail to make a full shoulder turn, you might not come through the ball smoothly, or perhaps you will not finish with your hands high, pointed in the direction of your target. During stressful circumstances, the same thing happens to your breathing. It typically becomes quick and there is a tendency to take shallow or incomplete breaths. In moments of extreme stress, some individuals go so far as to hold their breath. Consider the in and out, back and forth, pendulum-like similarities of breathing and the golf swing. It's no wonder that improper timing and rhythm can yield such destructive consequences in both cases of physical activity.

Shallow, hastened breathing is commonly referred to as hyperventilation. When experiencing a case of the nerves, you will automatically begin to hyperventilate and you most probably will have no awareness of doing so. Rapid breathing is part of the fight-or-flight response and is designed to get more oxygen to large muscle groups. The tendency toward shallow breathing, however, brings about the opposite effect. The supply of oxygen in the blood is reduced, which results in an increased need to "suck air."

Another by-product of nervous breathing is referred to as vasoconstriction. Because of increased activity in your flip-flopping stomach, blood flow gets redirected to the center of your body and the blood vessels that lead to the outer extremities become narrowed or vasoconstricted. Hands and feet become cold and a tingling or rubbery sensation may develop in your arms and legs. The head is also far from your body's core, and the blood vessels leading to the upper portion of your body become vasoconstricted as well. This can possibly lead to lightheadedness or, when taken to an extreme, a migraine headache. Add to the physiological havoc that is generated by irregular breathing, the mind's nervous reaction to these unpleasant sensations, and it is easy to see why the proper regulation of breathing is so critical to golf-course stress management.

Referred to as either a cleansing or diaphragmatic breath, healthy breathing results in a full and regular exchange of *all* the air in your lungs. This allows for the arrival of freshly oxygenated air which can work its way into your bloodstream, keeping you alert with muscles strong enough to perform efficiently.

The best way to know whether you are taking a full and healthy breath is by placing your hands on your abdomen. When you breathe in, what happens? Does your stomach expand or does it flatten out? If you are breathing with adequate depth, your stomach will expand, allowing for the arrival of new air that is being inhaled. It might be helpful to imagine your torso as being pear-shaped. Visualize the air you inhale as passing right past the narrower upper portion of your body and planting itself in the broader-based lower portion of the pear. As you exhale, your stomach (or the base of the pear) should flatten out. Push down on your stomach as you breathe out. This will exaggerate the feel of a proper cleansing breath and also help force out the deoxygenated air that you want your body to expel.

On the golf course, breathing provides the most immediate way to lessen the effects of autonomic activity, calm a sense of panic, and slow down thoughts that are racing. Just having the technique available becomes a tool that could serve the purpose of distracting you from the immediate source of your nervousness. Imagine, for instance, that you are on the green at the 17th hole of a tight match. You are one up on your opponent who is in the process of studying a straight five-foot par putt. You too will be putting for par, and although your putt is only two and a half feet, you are facing some downhill slope. Instead of staring at the ball marker and "catastrophizing" the potential outcome of the match, there exists a wonderful opportunity to employ the power of breathing. Turn away from your opponent, step off to the side of the green, stare at some pleasant scenery or, if you'd prefer, close your eyes. Then proceed to take two or three deep, anti-anxiety, cleansing breaths. After you have accomplished this, begin the study of your putt.

Don't Forget to Breathe

DESPITE THE FACT THAT I PREACH THE IMPORTANCE OF PROPER
breathing to patients and audiences on a regular basis, it is
entirely possible for me to exit the golf course after a frustrating,
anxiety-filled round, and suddenly have it hit me. I forgot to take
cleansing breaths. Even a seasoned pro like Curtis Strange has
stated, "Under pressure, one of the most important things I have
to remember to do is breathe."

One method that usefully provides a reminder for proper
breathing is referred to as a *cue*. A cue refers to any physical
symbol that represents an activity you wish to be reminded
about. In order to be effective, a cue should be situated in a place
that will not escape your attention. An example of a well-placed
cue for breathing might be a "B" written on the back of your golf
glove, on the top of the grip of each golf club, or on the side of
your bag. Each time you view the cue, you remember to take a
cleansing breath.

The best way to guarantee proper breathing on the golf course
is to make the cleansing breath a part of your preshot routine.
As you stand behind your ball and eye the target, let a deep
breath be the last thing you do before you step into the shot. As
you inhale and exhale, imagine the rhythm you want to employ
when you swing the club. This practice will enable you to relax
your body and at the same time, rehearse the pacing that will
most likely result in a fluid golf swing.

The use of proper breathing in all stressful situations—not just
on the golf course, but at home and work as well—will also
allow the practice to become a well-ingrained habit that will not
be easily forgotten. So when you find yourself facing one of
those gut-check moments on the golf course—you won't have
to think about it—the cleansing breath will be an automatic
response.

Learning to Relax

RELAXATION, PARTICULARLY IN TIMES OF STRESS, DOES NOT COME
naturally to most, and it is not a technique that can necessarily
be summoned upon demand. To the contrary, relaxation is a skill

that, in order to be mastered, must be understood, learned, and diligently practiced.

Muscle tension is one of the predominant consequences of the anxiety that accompanies autonomic activity. The shoulders, neck, stomach, arms, and legs all begin to tighten in stressful situations. And as is the case with all physical signs of anxiety, the mind's interpretation of this bodily reaction serves to intensify it. The goal of relaxation training is to break this mind-body cycle. The theory behind relaxation training contends that if your body is relaxed, your mind will similarly interpret the situation you are in as being a relaxed state of affairs. Simply stated, relaxation theory is based on the notion that a relaxed body is incompatible with a fearful mind-set.

The following routine, known as progressive relaxation, is a popular and well-proven method for accomplishing a relaxed bodily state.

1. Find a comfortable and quiet place to sit or lie down. To enable proper blood flow, do not cross your arms or legs. Make sure that you are not wearing any constrictive clothing. Give yourself a minimum of ten minutes to fully perform the technique.

2. Close your eyes and take two cleansing breaths. As you exhale, feel the tension leaving your body. Next, proceed to scan your body in a head-to-toe fashion, searching for specific areas of tension. You will systematically relax your muscle groups until your entire body is free from tension. Some individuals find it useful to first tense their muscles before relaxing them. This creates a sense of contrast that helps in achieving a fully relaxed state.

3. Begin with the muscles in your scalp and face. Release all the tension in this area of your body. If effectively carried out, your lips should part slightly. If your eyes remain open, your vision will become blurred.

4. Proceed through your neck, down through your shoulders, and down the length of your arms. Your arms should begin to feel either heavy or weightless—as if they have become a part of the arms of your chair. Think of your arms as rag dolls. If they were lifted and released, they would fall

immediately. Flutter your fingers (the way divers and
swimmers do before competition). Feel and visualize blood
flowing down your arms into your fingers. It might be useful to visualize tiny gates within your wrists opening to
allow the blood flow to increase to your hands. After a
couple of minutes, you should notice your hands becoming
warmer. Picture all the stress from your upper body shooting down the length of your arms—like lightning bolts—
and flying out of your body through the tips of your fingers.

5. Continue your downward path of progressive relaxation by
   returning to your chest. Take another cleansing breath, and
   as you exhale, notice the tension and tightness leaving your
   upper body. Proceed to your stomach—a very common
   "seat" of tension—and relieve all the tension from this portion of your body.

6. As you travel past your hips, relax your legs in the same
   manner you did with your arms. They too should become
   "rag doll" heavy, with the image of blood flowing down
   through your thighs and shins, into your feet. In your
   ankles, visualize the opening of the same tiny gates that you
   envisioned in your wrists. Imagine all lower-body stress
   shooting down your legs and flying out of the tips of your
   toes. At this point, you should notice your feet beginning
   to feel warm.

7. When you have reached the bottom of your body, take another deep breath, and quickly scan your entire body, once
   again in head-to-toe fashion. Spend a good five minutes in
   this final relaxed state before you conclude the exercise.

Relaxing on the Golf Course

RELAXATION TECHNIQUES OBVIOUSLY CANNOT BE PRACTICED IN
their entirety during a round of golf. Unless you're Bill Murray,
the practice of lying down on the tee area or around the green
and going through this technique would probably be considered
inappropriate. There are, however, "portable" methods that
make use of an abbreviated technique called *differential relaxation*.
This refers to the practice of relieving the tension only in the

parts of your body that are required for a particular task. These can be performed without bringing any attention to yourself and they can be accomplished in a matter of seconds.

Before differential relaxation can be learned, it is necessary to put some time into the full-scale version of progressive relaxation. If you have maintained a schedule for practicing this technique, you understand the "rag doll" feel of relaxed arms and legs. Once this learning has occurred, you will in a matter of seconds be able to relieve the specific or differential tension in the shoulders, arms, and legs—the muscle groups most central to a smooth, unhampered golf swing. You can bypass the rigor of a head-to-toe muscle scan, and simply release the necessary muscles as you are in the exhale phase of a cleansing breath. When successfully accomplished, you will feel your shoulders drop, arms fall relaxed by your sides, and your knees buckle slightly. You will now be ready for a powerful and fully extended golf swing.

As was true with proper breathing technique, it is also easy to *forget* to relax during anxious moments. You can again employ a cue to remind yourself to release bodily tension. Young LPGA star Kelly Robbins makes use of her father's suggestion that she "think about catching a nice fish" during high-pressure situations. This relaxing image reminds her to release the potentially destructive bodily tension that she is no doubt experiencing when the heat is on. It didn't take Ms. Robbins long to "reel in a big one," when she birdied three of the final seven holes to rally past Laura Davies and earn a one-stroke victory in the 1995 LPGA Championship.

Cues are essential for remembering to step back and take stock of the situation and to keep your nerves in check during critical moments of play. The *best* way to guarantee that you remember to relax is to make the release of tension in your arms, shoulders, and legs a part of your preshot routine. Ideally, the cleansing breath and differential relaxation technique should be learned in tandem and incorporated into the routine you follow before every single shot. The more frequently you practice the breathing-relaxing response, the more your body will have "memorized" this skill. You will also be in a much better position to handle all forms of typical as well as unexpected stressful events that occur both on the golf course and in the course of your daily life.

The Power of Self-Hypnosis

YOU WILL RECALL THAT HAZARD ONE GOLFERS, IN ADDITION TO being sensitive to physiological activity, also have active, analytical, impressionable minds. When Arnie heard the voice of the "devil," it was actually his own thoughts and fears helping to complete the self-destruction of his confidence. While the techniques of proper breathing and progressive relaxation do a good job of reducing the body's reactions to autonomic activities, these irrational, panic-filled thoughts still need to be examined and controlled.

Self-hypnosis is a technique that combines the forces of breathing and relaxation with the alteration of self-destructive patterns of thinking. This last component is known as cognitive restructuring. The basic premise behind this technique is that thoughts, to a great extent, control emotions. For instance, while in the middle of a substandard round, you are probably making negative statements to yourself. These thoughts are processed by your subconscious as being true, resulting in a snowballing, self-fulfilling pattern of despair and poor play. Cognitive restructuring refers to the process of consciously imposing positive self-statements designed to replace these less rational, more destructive thoughts that initially race through your mind.

Self-hypnosis is a powerful technique that addresses all levels of the Hazard One response. It is based on the understanding that when the body is relaxed, the subconscious mind is more receptive to incoming messages. Positive, self-affirming statements, listened to while the body is in a relaxed state, slip beyond conscious awareness, and are stored at the subconscious level. During the heat of competition, when you need them most, these positive statements will involuntarily take the form of thoughts that will have an impact on golf performance.

Suppose that you are to play an important match in the evening and are becoming increasingly nervous during the day. Self-hypnosis can be used to calm you down to a productive level of arousal. In addition, you could anticipate tense moments that might come up during the round, and impose positive outcomes on them at the subconscious level. During the actual round, you will feel much calmer and more confident than if you had just let your body and mind run freely.

As is true for relaxation, self-hypnosis must be practiced away from the golf course. Instead of actually using the technique or portions of the technique on the golf course, self-hypnosis will prewire you to react and think in a positive manner when you are in the actual situation. To practice self-hypnosis, you will need approximately ten minutes, during which time you will first perform your progressive relaxation technique. Once in a calm, relaxed state, you will listen to positive statements about your subsequent golf performance. These affirmative messages could be delivered as thoughts, or more effectively, they can be tape-recorded and listened to. Most individuals have some degree of difficulty remembering positive cognitions while in an anxious state and do better with the tape recordings. You could develop one or several tapes that you use regularly. To reinforce the self-hypnotic exercise, you could listen to the tape in the car, on your way to the golf course. The contents might be as follows:

One swing at a time. I'm going to take my time, go through my routine, and put all my concentration into each individual stroke. Everyone will be nervous on the first tee tonight, and no one will be focusing their attention on me. If I feel myself getting nervous, I will take a cleansing breath, and relax my shoulders, arms, and legs. I will remember that I am very sensitive and will probably feel some physical signs of nervousness. So long as I don't react fearfully to these physical changes, they will quickly pass and be replaced by calm, alert, and energized feelings. I will remind myself that this is only a game and that I'm out here to have fun. I might win the match or I might lose it, but I know that I will bear down on each and every shot, and accept the results.

Because of your relaxed state, this message will slip into your subconscious, where it will be drawn upon later in the day. In fact, after ten minutes of practicing this technique, it is doubtful that you will experience anything more than some mild anxiety for the rest of the day. You will look forward to playing and be less worried about the outcome.

Into the Teeth of Fear

IF YOU PRACTICE AND EMPLOY THE TECHNIQUES FOR CONTROLLING anxiety, you will be in a good position to overcome your nervousness and perform effectively. There will, however, remain one small matter that will still need to be accomplished. That is, the business of actually facing your fear. That moment of truth when you dive straight into the teeth of your fear and actually experience the source of your anxiety.

My moment came at the start of my third full season as a golfer. I had reached a point in my game where I felt competent enough to play along with most other golfers and not stand out on the basis of poor play. The problem was that I was playing with a very small circle of compassionate, nonthreatening friends who had seen me through the tough times. Whenever I was hooked up with strangers, or a friend brought along someone I didn't know, I could feel my anxiety level turn up a notch. My Hazard One control methods worked just fine, but only under very limited conditions.

When the offer to fill a vacant slot in a golf league came up, I was very reluctant to take the plunge. Excuses such as "I'm not ready," or "It won't be fair to the other players," were only designed to cover up my anxiety about playing under pressure, in unfamiliar circumstances, with people I did not know. The tingling in my arms and queasiness in my stomach that resulted from just thinking about it sent me the loud and clear signal that league play was exactly what I needed to do.

I have been on live television countless times and have addressed rooms filled with hundreds of people, but I do not recall ever experiencing the case of nerves I had during the day of my first ever league match. Standing on the first tee plays back in my memory like a dream, or perhaps more like a nightmare. I vaguely recall shaking hands with other league members and going through the motion of stretching while looking around for a water fountain. My cotton mouth was accompanied by rubbery legs, a pulsating neck, and the strong desire to slip away, change my phone number, and perhaps, if necessary, move to a different state.

As luck would have it, I was a member of the first foursome out and was thereby afforded the luxury of having a full audience for my tee shot. I accepted the reality that my anxiety was too far gone to be regulated by cleansing breaths, progressive relaxation, or cognitive restructuring. I was a "runaway freight train"—too far into the fight-or-flight response—to even think about calming down.

When the first player finally hit his tee shot, I noticed our league's "first-tee jester" positioned along the tee markers, ready to offer commentary regarding the outcome of everyone's tee shot. My turn to hit; I turned to him with my most pleading face of innocence and vulnerability, praying that he might show some mercy on the rookie. I don't know how I managed to make any contact with the ball at all, but I somehow popped it up, straight out, about 130 yards into the fairway. The jester smiled at me and said, "Nice nine-iron." I inhaled my first dose of oxygen in several minutes and replied with all the sincerity in the world, "I'll take it." Even though I took a 9 on the par-four first hole, I didn't care. I eventually settled down and played some decent golf, even making a match out of it (it didn't hurt to get 8 handicap strokes for 9 holes). After I lipped out a three-footer on 9 to lose the match, I ran to my car, swallowed three extra-strength aspirin, and joined the boys for a beer.

My problems with Hazard One stayed with me for the first half of the league's season. Each week, as Wednesday approached, I felt myself getting worked up again. I dealt with it by practicing more and continuing to utilize the techniques for overcoming Hazard One. It eventually came around for me and I even managed at one point to reel off eight consecutive victories. Going into the final week, I was actually in a position to win the B Flight. My golf game had improved along with my self-esteem. The techniques for controlling anxiety helped me get through the experience, but what I felt best about was the fact that I faced a situation *despite* my feelings of anxiety.

I am well into my third season as a member of the same league, and although I will confess to some mild butterflies on the first tee, I currently consider myself a graduate of the Hazard

One school of self-destruction. I have seen it all. I have had my best and my worst rounds, have hit my best and my worst drives off the first tee, and I have seen everyone else in the league do the same. Our first-tee jester is still planted at his station, but I have come to enjoy the challenge of his presence. And on those days when I hit a poor drive, I pick up my tee, accept his dig, and head up the fairway laughing.

The techniques outlined in this chapter are excellent tools for managing the anxiety you will experience when you take the plunge into a nerve-racking situation. But even the finest tools serve no purpose if they are not used. Whether it be the phobic individual who experiences anxiety while driving or getting on an airplane, or the golfer who feels the pinch in tournament play or when there's money on the line, the situation eventually *must be faced* if it is ever to be overcome. Make use of the Hazard One techniques for getting through the early stages of your golf anxiety. Then watch yourself become calmer and more self-assured to the point where you can leave your tools at home, secure in the knowledge that within you lies the courage to avoid living a life that is controlled by your fears.

4

HAZARD TWO:
Losing Your Cool

"Anger is never without a reason, but
seldom with a good one."

—BENJAMIN FRANKLIN

*The 7-iron suspended in the middle branches of the large maple
adjacent to the green on the 12th hole served as testimony to Tom
Wilson's potential for enraged outbursts. Everyone at the club knew
Tom, and most members made every effort to avoid playing with
him.*

*In this particular instance, Tom had attempted to pitch and run
one from the rough, across the wide, two-tiered green, but his flub
only managed to advance the ball a couple of feet forward into still
deeper rough. This in itself might not have resulted in the toss of the
7-iron. It was more likely his approach shot that was responsible for
the club finding a place in the old maple. After hitting a perfect
240-yard drive right down the middle of the fairway, Tom proceeded
to hit a 4-iron so fat that his divot actually managed to gain more
distance than the ball. This was followed by a skulled 5-iron to the
rough just under the farthest extended branches of the big maple
tree.*

*But perhaps we need to go back even further in Tom's day to fully
understand how his 7-iron ended up in the maple. Tom had a meeting
with his regional manager that day to review sales numbers for the
past two quarters. Everyone knew that his company's retail sales for
men's sportswear had been knocked off stride by the competition.*

Tom was scared that after seventeen years with the same company, he could find himself out of a job.

So that morning when Tom's wife and teenage daughter brought their battle to the kitchen—going at it about everything from the appropriateness of her clothing to her curfew next Saturday night— Tom could not help but react. All he wanted to do was read the sports section, relax and prepare for the bear of a day that awaited him. But it was not to be. So when his daughter left the house, he made one simple comment to his wife: "Why do you let her push your buttons like that? You take the bait every time." And one simple comment was all that was required to send Tom and his wife into a full-blown, hateful shouting match, and then send Tom out the door, into his workday with a wicked headache and a sick feeling in the pit of his gut.

Two blocks from his office, waiting at an intersection, watching the light change three times didn't help any. And when the regional sales manager, with spreadsheets and graphs, clearly demonstrated the 27 percent decline in Tom's sales productivity over the past two quarters, all Tom could think about was his 5:04 P.M. tee-time. A peaceful feeling, an excitement came over him. He would deal with these problems tomorrow. Today, what he needed was to escape it all. And what could be more perfect than nine holes on a beautiful summer night.

And so you have the tale that goes with the legend of the dangling 7-iron on 12. There is no question that Tom needed an escape after his stress-packed day. But somehow, Tom's plan failed miserably. Rather than escape the internal rage he had experienced for most of the day, he brought it with him to the golf course. This is a perfectly commonplace event, since those who struggle with anger in the course of their everyday lives also have a propensity to lose their cool in response to the frustration that is a fact of life for anyone on a golf course.

Hazard Two Characteristics

EVERYONE KNOWS A GOLFER LIKE TOM, AND EVERYONE CAN AP-preciate how golf—with its minuscule margin for error and lengthy periods of downtime—is probably the most frustrating game in the world. Add to this frustration the fact that golf is a no contact, no run, dive, jump, or slide sport, which does not permit the release of physical tension, and this leaves the Hazard Two golfer ready to explode. Even if you don't bend clubs over your knee or throw them into water hazards, you have no doubt had many moments in golf that tested your frustration-tolerance level. Everyone has. But how you reacted to the negative thoughts and feelings that you experienced during these instances was—whether you realized it or not—a function of how well you understood and managed your anger.

Much like anxiety, anger is a genetically implanted fact of evolution that produces physiological changes necessary for survival in times of threat. Your heart will pound, your stomach turn, and blood will be delivered to the large muscle groups to enhance the ability to attack the source of your threat. The primary difference between the autonomic reaction of anxiety and that of anger is that anxiety attack sufferers are typically in flight mode while angry people are ready to step in and fight.

With anxiety, you play the victim, oftentimes not understanding the bodily changes you are experiencing, and often at a loss to know what to do about them. With anger, although you are reacting to very similar physiological changes, you know (or at least think you know) why you are angry, and rather than feel as if you are being attacked, feel the need to initiate an attack. This is why anger is a less petrifying emotion than anxiety. There exists with anger a feeling of being in control. But when all is said and done, you are anything but in control. By *losing* your cool, you have also lost your rhythm and your ability to think clearly and focus. You have lost the time-suspended, childlike feelings of joy that the game can evoke. And you have very likely lost the respect of your playing partners.

If it is true that anger is a survival reaction which is elicited by some type of personal or territorial threat, what could possibly pose such a threat on the golf course? The answer is that Hazard Two golfers are *always* threatened by something. They might be threatened by co-workers, by the driver who inadvertently cuts them off, by what they might regard as an inconsiderate or insensitive friend or member of the family. The terrain that Hazard Twos need to protect goes beyond the sustenance of food, money, and the shelter of a home. For the terrain of the Hazard Two individual is built on the fertile soil of ego and pride. And the substandard golf outing presents a threat to this most sensitive of territories.

Self-Esteem vs. Golf-Esteem

THERE IS NOTHING LIKE THOSE DAYS WHEN YOU JUST CAN'T MISS. Days when drives are consistently "on the screws," unexpected kicks and bounces are friendly, and putts rim the cup and drop straight down. It's so easy to be pleasant on such days—to offer support to struggling partners, to pick up the tab on the 19th hole. And why not? Feel good about yourself, lap it up, fully relish the moment! If you can't bask in the splendor of days like these, why play the game at all?

It's a little tougher, on the other hand, to feel good and be pleasant on days when *you* are the one who's struggling. This is entirely understandable and to a great extent, even acceptable. It all comes down to the degree to which you react and the extent to which these reactions impact on the people you are socializing with. No one at his club wanted to play with Tom. Could you blame them? Why should *his* game be so important as to take center stage and dominate the day's events?

If you are a Hazard Two golfer your problems extend beyond your temper tantrums on the golf course. Whether you want to admit it to yourself or not, you have a problem with self-esteem and you invest too much of your identity into your golf game. Because you question your basic self-worth in many areas of your life, you have created in golf an opportunity to believe that you do in fact measure up. Tom couldn't wait to get out to play on the eve of his stress-filled day. His objective was simple escape. However, his needs were more complex than he thought. After a day of feeling judged and not living up to his *own* expectations for success and positive self-worth, he hoped that success on the golf course would create the positive feelings he so desperately craved. When he failed to play well, his disappointment was devastating. His poor play only reinforced the belief that he was a loser of little worth.

If you haven't tossed this book across the room yet, there exists the hope that you are ready to stop lying to yourself and to come to grips with the reality that your rage on the golf course is inappropriate and stems from personal issues that extend well beyond the scope of your golf game. You do not want to gain legendary status among your playing peers in the manner that Tom did. And you know that your frustration and anger in response to poor play only make your game suffer more. The remaining portions of this chapter will outline methods for managing your anger on the golf course. To effectively deal with the problem in other areas of your life, however, you'll need to keep working on building self-esteem well after you've read the last page of this book.

What Are You Really Mad About?

TOM'S TOSSED 7-IRON WAS THE CLIMAX TO A SERIES OF INSTANCES that frustrated and threatened him. The following example will illustrate how anger builds up in a cumulative manner. Imagine a reservoir that looks like a clear beaker located inside your stomach. Picture a yellow line etched one inch from the top of this container. Further imagine that every time you experience anger without expressing it, a red liquid is poured into this beaker. You will recall that Tom began his day anticipating his meeting with his boss. Before he even stepped out into the world, the base of his beaker was already covered with the red fluid. Add two inches for the fight with his wife, another inch for the traffic on the way to work, two more inches for the meeting with his boss, another inch for his worried thoughts about losing his job after this meeting, a half-inch for the fat 4-iron, another half for the skulled 5-iron, and the final half for the flubbed 7-iron, bringing the red fluid over the yellow line. Having exceeded his threshold for internalizing frustration, Tom had little choice but to lose his cool.

Whenever you feel rage—at a co-worker or spouse, in the car, or on the golf course—it is extremely critical that you ask yourself the question: *What am I really mad about?* More often than not, you have distorted the legitimate source of your frustration and anger. I recently worked with a patient who demonstrates this point. Sarah was a 35-year-old career woman, married with two children, and concerned that her husband, Carl, was no longer the right man for her.

> *I don't know what it is about Carl. When I'm driving home from work and thinking about him, I tell myself that he's a great guy, that I'm lucky to have someone like him. But the second I walk in the door and see his face, something inside of me clicks and I can't stomach anything about him. He seems like such a jerk. I appreciate the fact that he's gotten dinner started, but he always screws something up. Either he forgot to put up the baked potatoes, or he maybe left the oven on when he was done with it. And he's so disorganized. The kitchen looks like a bomb hit it. Every light in the house is on, he doesn't know if the kids began their homework, and you can be certain that he forgot to check the mail. And he greets me with this stupid expression on his face. I can't help it. As soon as I step foot in the door, I want to turn around and leave.*

Do you think Sarah's impressions of her husband were more valid when she was thinking about him, on her way home from work, or when she stepped into her home? Sarah had a tough, pressure-filled job. During the course of her workday, she had to smile at idiots and tolerate criticism from superiors who knew less than she did. All day long, wearing a pleasant social face, Sarah's beaker was filling up. Poor Carl happened to be there when the red liquid exceeded the yellow line. In and of itself, this is not necessarily a problem. The problem with Sarah was that she *believed* that Carl was the enemy, that he was the *cause* of her foul mood. Fortunately for Sarah and her family, she was open to the truth about her misplaced anger and eventually came to appreciate her husband's efforts to be supportive.

And so it goes with golf. When Tom flubbed the pitch with his 7-iron, he had no clue that his beaker had been filling up since the beginning of the day. In his mind, the reason he threw his 7-iron was that he was frustrated about not playing up to his potential. If Tom was able to put it all in perspective, if he was capable of recognizing that his personal and professional lives were wrought with insecurities and self-doubt, that golf *was not* his problem, several positive outcomes could have potentially occurred.

For one, Tom could have started delving into his nongolf problems and begun the process of "getting his house in order." By expecting less from himself on that summer evening, he probably would have performed better and he certainly would have enjoyed himself more. The problems Tom faced during the day were not going to go away regardless of how well or poorly he played on that beautiful summer night. He could have anticipated his tee-time comforted by the knowledge that the wonderful game of golf would present him with an opportunity to escape and recover from the stress of this horrible day, recharged and ready to deal with his *real* problems on the following day.

Nip It in the Bud with the "Three Rs"

THE BEST WAY TO GUARANTEE THAT YOU ARE NOT IMPAIRED BY THE buildup of anger is to nip it in the bud—that is, to avoid the accumulation of anger by developing a method for *recovering* from stress in regular intervals. By consciously taking the time to intermittently express pent-up anger and keep your red fluid comfortably beneath the yellow threshold line, you will effectively manage to avoid the "out-of-control," fitful rage.

Each time you face an anger-provoking situation, your heart starts racing, your stomach begins to churn, and your body burns oxygen at a faster rate. Because anger, in a manner similar to anxiety, activates the physiological changes that are a part of the fight-or-flight response, the intermittent practice of proper breathing and of releasing muscular tension, detailed in the previous chapter, is also very effective for the management of anger.

The cleansing breath, along with the practice of relaxation, can be used to employ the "Three Rs" technique for management of anger. To illustrate how this process works, let's go back to the case of Tom. He is once again sitting at the breakfast table, hearing his wife and daughter argue. Rather than allow his anger to escalate, Tom will *recognize, reduce, and reenter* the situation. First, he *recognizes* that he is under a good deal of stress and "freeze-frames" his life for a moment at the breakfast table. Second, he *reduces* bodily stress by taking a cleansing breath and doing a quick head-to-toe scan to relax muscular tension. Third, he *reenters* the situation he was in. In this case, he goes back to his newspaper, feeling calmer and not so wired to react. By momentarily stopping his life for that moment at the breakfast table, Tom, in effect, got away from himself. Consider how often you feel the need to get away from everyone and everything yet feel helpless to do so. Despite your feelings of entrapment during these unpleasant moments, the Three-Rs method provides an escape route. A cleansing breath, a burst of fresh oxygen, released muscular tension, and at least for a brief moment in time, things will not seem all that unmanageable.

Cognitive Restructuring

THE TECHNIQUE OF COGNITIVE RESTRUCTURING REFERS TO THE conscious replacing of irrational, negative thoughts, with healthier and more positive inner speech. It is based on the theory that negative thoughts are responsible for generating negative emotions. To make use of cognitive restructuring for avoiding the buildup of anger, it is important that you learn how to *slow things down* during stressful circumstances. The Three Rs can be useful for snapping you back into reality and providing you with the opportunity to restructure angry and irrational thoughts into calmer and more positive self-statements. A pressure-packed moment on the golf course will help demonstrate the power of positive versus negative self-talk.

You are on the tee of one of the latter holes of an important match. You have just three-putted the prior hole as well as three of the last six. Moments ago, in response to your frustration, you tossed your ball into the woods, and can still feel yourself reeling from the intensity of your anger and self-disdain. Consider the following list of alternative messages you can present to yourself during this acutely stressful moment.

POSITIVE SELF-TALK	NEGATIVE SELF-TALK
What do I need to accomplish at this moment?	I have to nail this drive or I'm dead!
Stay calm, this is not life or death.	I'll be so depressed if I lose this match.

| What's done is done. One shot at a time. | If any of those putts fell, this match would be wrapped up right now. |
| A couple of cleansing breaths, relax, and I'll be fine. | I'm tight as a drum! I can't wait to get this over with. |

The difference between the positive and the negative self-talking golfer could very well be the difference in the match. Because the body listens to the mind, the conscious imposition of uplifting, positive thoughts relaxes the body to the point where it performs naturally, unimpaired by the critical, self-doubting comments arriving from "central control."

This concept was cleverly presented by W. Timothy Gallwey in his book *The Inner Game of Golf.* He describes two identities, *Self 1* and *Self 2*, who reside within the golfer's mind. Self 2 operates on the basis of unspoken self-trust and simply goes about the business of playing golf. Self 1 plays the role of critic and is quick to point out past errors and suggest the high probability that these errors will be repeated. When the critical voice of Self 1 is in charge, performance suffers. With Self 2 at the helm, play is effortless and highly effective. This is where the technique of cognitive restructuring and positive self-talk is so valuable. By using the Three Rs, slowing things down, and imposing positive self-statements during moments of anger-building frustration, a calm and collected Self 2 will be swinging the golf club for you.

Try Self-Hypnosis

IF WHILE IN THE HEAT OF BATTLE YOU CANNOT NECESSARILY TRUST yourself to "stop the world" in order to breathe, relax, and think positively, you are well advised to consider the employment of self-hypnosis in your arsenal of Hazard Two management techniques. Before you go out to the course, go through the procedure that was outlined in Chapter 3. While practicing the progressive relaxation method, listen to a tape-recorded message designed to counter your usual repertoire of anger-inducing thoughts. The following can serve as an example:

I know there are going to be lots of frustrating moments out there. This is a fact of golf, not just for me, but for everyone. I know that once I "lose it," it's hard for me to get it back. That's why I've got to remain cool and avoid going over the edge. Even if I hit a tee shot out-of-bounds or miss a simple putt, I will not react with anger. Instead, I will take a deep breath, relax my shoulders and arms, and tell myself that the only shot that counts is the next shot. Then I will put all my energy and concentration into that next shot. There'll be a lot of golf to be played, and I'll have plenty of opportunities to make up for mistakes. Most important, I will be pleasant to be around and I will enjoy the day. I will not lose myself to anger.

If you are serious about your desire to stop losing your cool, self-hypnosis *will* work. You will find that when you face a critical moment that tests you, on or off the golf course, the calm voice of reason that you listened to during your hypnotic session will be there. At first, you will be amazed at the power you have to change your negative thinking and miserable behavior. You will feel grateful to have finally found a tool that is well defined and easy to employ, one that actually helps neutralize your hot temper. And you will be grateful to have taken another major step in your struggle to put an end to the self-destructive golf round.

Find Someone You Can Talk To

WHEN I AM IN MY ROLE AS A PSYCHOLOGIST, WORKING WITH AN individual who struggles with the management of anger, I suggest the mind and body techniques that are discussed in this chapter. I also encourage the development of insight into issues that pertain to self-esteem. And I listen. It is while in the role of listener that I am enabling the patient to let off steam, to have an outlet for expressing the rage that is bottled up within.

You do not have to see a psychologist to express whatever it is that ails you. A spouse, a friend, any acquaintance that you feel comfortable with and have regular access to, will suffice in the role of sounding board and confidante. Are you really pissed off about the corrupt nature of government spending? Fed up with political correctness? Hate lawyers, banks, and insurance companies? Hate people? Hate yourself?!

Get it off your chest by *honestly* expressing it to someone you trust. Not just anyone, but someone who you believe cares about how you feel and what you have to say. It takes only one person to serve this purpose. But, if you have no one—not a spouse, friend, counselor, clergyman—that you can talk to on a regular basis, you are going to suffer the consequences of this basic human need that is missing from your life.

You would be wise to think about the people you know, and consider which of these relationships can perhaps be developed. Let it be a golfing buddy. Instead of just playing together, suggest lunch after or before a round. And don't just talk about the game of golf. Talk about how you *feel* when you play golf. About how angry, miserable, and worthless you feel when you struggle. You might even be so bold as to talk about how you feel when you're not playing golf. Just make it a point to express your perspective and feelings to someone, anyone on this planet. If you believe that there is no one who could serve in this role, it might be time to consider seeking out some professional help. This should provide you with a temporary outlet for expressing your rage, as well as with some ideas and support for branching your need for interpersonal communication beyond the constraints of the therapeutic relationship.

See the Humorous Side

HEALTH PROFESSIONALS HAVE LONG REALIZED THAT HUMOR IS good for the mind, body, and soul. Those individuals who have the ability to step outside of themselves and see the humor in their predicament have the advantage of not taking their lives too seriously. Most matters are not life and death, and even those that are can be helped along by seeing the humorous side. In his book, *Anatomy of an Illness*, Norman Cousins attributed part of his successful recovery from a life-threatening illness to watching *Candid Camera* reruns. So even when circumstances are a matter of life and death, the ability to laugh can help you get through it.

Hazard Two individuals tend to be cynical types who often

use humor to put others down or to form an allegiance with a Hazard Two compatriot who also derives benefit from the put-down of others. This is normal behavior for school-age children, who lift their own downtrodden self-esteems by indulging in the ego destruction of some unfortunate classmate, but you would think that mature adults would know better. The trouble is that many adults are not mature enough to know better. Cynical, sadistic humor might not necessarily be inappropriate when it is occasional, and so long as it is seen for what it really is. It is important to recognize that when you put down others, you are engaging in what psychologists refer to as *projection*. While employing this ego-protecting defense mechanism, you take on the role of a projector and others become the screen. You actually believe that what you observe in other people is a part of *their* character. In reality, you are observing qualities that you possess and are projecting—qualities that you don't like very much about yourself.

The golf course is a wonderful setting for poking fun at your-self. Where else do you behave in such a laughable manner? When your game is on, honestly believing that you have found the secret. When you lose it, worrying that you might never get it back. Feeling high as a kite in celebration of a great shot one instant, moments later slamming your clubhead into the turf in disgust with yourself. Don't you see it? Your behavior is laugh-able. You're being totally ridiculous and you don't even get it. Appreciate the fact that you *are* so passionate about your golf game. Just make sure to take an occasional moment to step back and observe yourself. And then laugh out loud at the character that is unmistakably you.

"Cool Mad"—When Anger Is Good

A COUPLE OF YEARS AGO, WHILE PLAYING A $2.00 NASSAU AGAINST an old golfing acquaintance, I found myself facing an interesting dilemma. It seemed that my opponent was pretty comfortable taking certain liberties with the interpretation of the rules, which I found a bit annoying. It was only a $2.00 Nassau, but I also remember Lee Trevino saying that taking a buck on a weekend outing from a friend had the satisfaction of a major victory. In other words, I wanted to win. Despite this desire, I refrained from commenting when he rolled his ball to improve his lie, when he grounded his wedge in a trap, and even when he took a couple of self-offered gimmes (those second putts after you've just missed which are quickly backhanded at the cup. If they go in, fine. If they miss, they don't count.). I decided to let it all go, just play my game, and allow my opponent to play his. I figured that sooner or later, I too would have a situation that would require the turning of the other cheek.

My moment arrived on the par-three 14th. A straight-ahead, nice, open 162-yard hole. Pin placed flush in the center of a relatively flat, moderately sized green. I took a lazy swipe at it with my 5-iron, resulting in a wimpy fade that carried a good 30 yards right, where it settled up against a fence. When I approached my ball, I saw that it had landed in a large puddle left by the heavy rains that had occurred over the past couple of days. Casual water, right? While my partner studied his birdie putt, I made the decision to give myself some relief. I chipped up, two-putted, content with my bogey.

Strolling toward the 15th tee, I was stunned by what occurred.

"I had a par, and you had a five," he stated, ready to record it on the scorecard.

Not a question, not a discussion, but a definitive statement.

"No I didn't," I defended myself. "I got a bogey."

"Didn't you take an unplayable by the fence?" he countered.

"My ball was in casual water. I was entitled to relief."

"But you were *against* the fence. You took relief from the water, but also advanced your ball away from the fence, closer to the hole. That should be a one-stroke penalty."

I'm not a stickler for the details on ruling, but as I thought about it, I figured that he probably was right. But I was not prepared to take a double on that hole. I tried a different approach. "We haven't exactly been playing up to USGA standards today. You've taken a few liberties yourself. I just let them go."

He looked like I attacked the basic essence of his character. "What are you talking about? I've been playing by the rules."

I needed that bogey. "What about rolling your ball?"

"You're crazy! I never touched my ball!"

"You grounded your club in the sand trap on eight."

"Now that I *know* I didn't do. I'm very aware of that rule. I *never* ground my club in a hazard." He looked sincerely hurt. As if he couldn't believe I could question his ethics.

Meanwhile, I began to seethe. How could I argue with him? I should have called him out when it was happening. But I didn't and he was being a jerk. He was a cheater, a clear and simple cheater and I hated his guts. It wasn't the money, of course. I already took the two bucks for the front side, was losing the back by maybe a couple of strokes, and was more than happy to give him a couple of dollars if he won the back and had the low total for 18. But I wasn't going to give my money to such a contemptible, lying, cheating, son of a mulligan.

"Forget it," I said. "Give me a five."

"Hey," he replied. "It's not a big deal to me. I'll give you the four. You're kicking my butt, anyway."

"GIVE ME A FIVE!" I exclaimed. "And also . . . let me take a look at that scorecard."

I had beaten him by two strokes on the front side; he had me by four (actually three) on the back. Four holes to play. I was absolutely determined to catch him. I was going to take his six bucks, shake his hand, and make it a point to never step onto a golf course with the miserable creep ever again.

I was hot and I was pumped and I played the last four holes in one over. I parred the next two holes, but it was my birdie against his triple on 17 that effectively finished him as I pulled to two ahead. When he lost his tee shot on 18, I relaxed and allowed myself to double-bogey the hole. But I am convinced that if he had played with me to that point, I would have pulled out a par to beat him.

Sam Snead calls it "cool mad." When you're angry enough to be pumped, using the surplus adrenaline to be focused and energized, yet remaining cool enough to stay cognizant of what you have to do to get the job done. I was definitely mad that day, and in my mentally exhausted state after the round, I tried to make sense of what had happened. I concluded that without planning it, my rage became my fuel, my motivation. While in the situation, I never stopped to question what I was doing. But after the fact, I realized that the experience taught me some valuable lessons about anger and about mental toughness.

If you are a Hazard Two golfer, recognize the force and power of your rage. Utilize the techniques and ideologies that were presented in this chapter to cool you down just enough to remain focused and be able to perform. On the other side of the matter, if you are not usually a particularly angry individual, and you are not playing all that well, find a reason to get angry. It could be the weather, your equipment, the condition of the course, or a playing partner such as my "friend." It doesn't matter what or whom you choose. A little anger during those low-energy, lackluster golf outings could be just the catalyst you need to become tougher mentally and to get back that zest in your swing.

5

HAZARD THREE:

Getting Too Up or Too Down

"When one door of happiness closes,
another opens; but often we look so long
at the closed door that we do not see the
one which has opened for us."

—HELEN KELLER

*Clarke hurried in the direction of his beautiful, clean, white Top-Flite,
sitting up nicely in the right-hand side of the fairway. His big drive
on the par-four, 372-yard 9th was positioned perfectly for his approach. When Clarke arrived at his ball—just short of the white
stake that served as the 150-yard marker—he looked up to see the
flag wave in the moderate left-to-right breeze. That pin was his for
the taking.*

*Clarke's opponent and longtime best friend had not experienced as
much good fortune off the tee at 9. With one hole to play and the
match all square, Jeff had tensed up and duck-hooked one smack into
the heart of the big willow. The dismal thwack of surlyn striking
bark signaled that the ball had not found its way through. At the
very best, Jeff would be looking at a chip-out.*

*You could hardly blame Clarke for being so excited. He was play-
ing the round of his life. The gap between his game and Jeff's had
narrowed considerably over the years, but somehow Jeff always found
a way to pull it out. But not today. Even if Jeff did manage to find
his ball, Clarke knew that he had finally taken one from his friend.*

*This is what it's all about, thought Clarke. To struggle, endure,
and eventually succeed. Over the course of their twelve-year friend-*

ship, Clarke had never beaten Jeff in a league match. And it was the twelve years of disappointment after disappointment that made it all the more satisfying. Clarke was actually happy it took so long. For this moment was rightfully his and no one could ever take it away from him.

Clarke relived the finish to that match again and again for the remainder of the golf season. His mind might replay it for the rest of his life. How Jeff managed to find his ball right behind the willow. How his choked-down punch with a 3-iron found its way through the willow's soft cascade of leaves, hooked onto the fairway, and rolled. And rolled. How it kept on rolling until it came to rest front and center of the green, about ten yards short of the front apron.

And there stood Clarke, out in the middle of the fairway, alone with his 6-iron. He glanced at Jeff, who wasn't exactly smiling, but had a smirky, self-satisfied look that Clarke recognized and knew only too well. When he waved his hand, motioning for Clarke to hit up, their eyes locked for an instant. Both he and Clarke knew the match was over.

Clarke lost a lot of his enthusiasm for the game for quite some time after that devastating loss. To Clarke, the match was less a victory for Jeff, than another choke by himself. Sure, Jeff made an incredible recovery shot and did manage to get up and down for a great scrambling par. But it wasn't even close. Clarke lost the hole and then some, and he couldn't get it out of his mind. He just couldn't bring himself to recover enough to find much pleasure in this cruel and heartless game.

Do you think that Clarke began his celebration a bit too early? In Clarke's mind the match had ended after his tee shot. He was no longer in a position to deal with any unexpected adversity. When Jeff pulled off his improbable recovery shot, Clarke had already rendered himself incapable of responding with a shot of his own.

Good, steady golf play requires not getting too up or too down. Jeff demonstrated this ability, and because of it, he pulled out the match. If Clarke did not fall prey to Hazard Three, *he* could have remained steady enough to compose himself after Jeff's brilliant recovery. He could have remained in a position to win that match.

Hazard Three Characteristics

HAZARD THREE GOLFERS ARE MOODY INDIVIDUALS WHO EXPERI-
ence a wide range of emotions in the course of their daily lives.
For some, there exists fluctuation in mood from one day to the
next. For others, the swing of moods can literally take place from
moment to moment. Traveling the breadth of emotions has the
potential to create a richness of experience that can be intensely
satisfying. However, as was the case with Hazard One and Hazard Two, how this hazard will affect your game depends on the
development of insight as well as the development of tools that
can help you manage this potentially self-destructive tendency.

Hazard One and Hazard Two are both associated with the
fight-or-flight response. The emotions of anxiety and anger are
based on an aroused, energized state designed to generate the
fortitude necessary for survival. When excessive and potentially
destructive, this energy can be toned down to a functional, even
productive level. As a Hazard Three golfer, your state of arousal
is typically anything but productive. You are either *too* high or
completely drained, left with no energy at all. If your survival
were threatened while you were in the down phase of your
moods, you would likely be a sitting duck. For when you are
disappointed in yourself, you feel immobilized, paralyzed, helpless, hopeless, and worthless.

There is a saying that you should never begin a day any more
fast-paced than you hope to finish it. This notion forms the basis
for the self-destructive experience that Hazard Three golfers are
all too familiar with. When Clarke began his early celebration,
complete with his body's release of euphoria-inducing chemicals, he was incapable of returning to an emotional midpoint.
When his opponent pulled off the unexpected, the bottom fell
out for Clarke. His premature euphoria had already drained his
body of the chemicals now required to climb out of the hole he
had dug for himself. He was too spent and exhausted to reach
back for the strength to fight.

Nothing More Than Feelings

WHEN I THINK BACK ON THE EARLY ROUNDS IN MY GOLFING CA-
reer, what most stands out to me is not how horribly inept I
was at the game, but rather how deeply depressed I became in
response to the frustration I experienced. I was mature enough
to realize that my feelings of shame, dejection, and sadness were
nothing short of ridiculous. But I couldn't help how I felt.

And there were still the superhigh moments of greatness that
occurred just often enough to counter the devastating lows.
Pharmaceutically pure heroin couldn't have addicted me any
more quickly than a drive down the middle of the fairway. It was
just a matter of sacrificing a bit of the manic rush in exchange for
a bit less emotional fallout.

By hacking away and literally suffering through some night-
marish rounds, I did manage to learn a few things about myself
and about people in general. I learned that when it comes to the
experiencing of feelings, there are basically two types of people.
The first type are those whose feelings and moods are based on
external circumstance. If the sun is shining, the family is well,
and there's no pressing work to be done, they are happy. For
these individuals, emotional reactions are derived on the basis
of objective reality.

Then, there are Hazard Three types, whose emotions run wild
and free, seemingly with a mind of their own. It is possible for a
Hazard Three to be lying on a sun-drenched beach in Bermuda,
a good book in one hand, and a strawberry daiquiri in the other,
and feel absolutely miserable. Conversely, they could be in the
midst of a stress-filled workday and experience rushes of joy.
The Hazard Three's emotions remain unpredictable and oftentimes out of control. Recognizing this, and understanding what
to do about it, is the first step in overcoming the self-destructive,
hazardous tendency of getting too up or too down.

As a Hazard Three, it is important to accept the fact that your
feelings are nothing more than fleeting and random signals that
fly past your conscious awareness. They have very little to do
with what your life's about. If after an ugly round you *feel* like a
loser with very little character, you are very simply wrong. On
the other hand, if you have the round of your life, and feel as if

you've discovered the secret to a repeating swing that will never again falter, you are also wrong. Once you come to understand how your emotions work, you will see that extreme feelings of either a negative or positive nature are seldom accurate. Such feelings are typically short-lived and, in retrospect, seem ludicrous.

As was true with Hazard Two golfers, Hazard Threes have a problem with low self-esteem. Feeling unworthy in the course of your daily life, you are quick to get very high or very low in response to golf performance. Smack the ball well and you're okay. Chunk, shank, or skull it and you're some kind of jerk. Makes life simple, doesn't it? As ridiculous as it might sound, consider the extent to which you actually engage in this pattern of thinking. If you are not dealing with life's core issues—those that pertain to faith, family, and work—you very well might be deluding yourself with the belief that success or failure in golf is what determines the strength of your character. Limited by the constraints of this finite volume, I leave these issues to your sense of conviction and purpose. And to the strength of your desire to live a life of honesty and authenticity.

Interpreting What You Feel

THERE ARE SEVERAL THEORIES THAT ATTEMPT TO EXPLAIN THE Hazard Three golfer's predicament. One theory suggests a genetic predisposition to moodiness that is associated with an imbalance in the brain's production of chemicals required to transmit neurological signals. Another theory advocates the notion that the tendency toward mood swings was developed by exposure to trauma, abuse, or dysfunctional parenting during critical and vulnerable phases of early childhood. Therefore, to a certain extent, moods are perhaps a function of an inborn personality trait or events that are well rooted in early experience. Along these lines, there might be limits to the extent that emotional highs and lows are readily amenable to change.

Another theory that offers an explanation for destructive mood fluctuations *does* allow for substantial progress in learning how to regulate these moods. Cognitive theory has to do with the manner in which you misread both your feelings and your thoughts and, as a result, create negative and oftentimes irrational self-statements. Hazard Three's often make this mistake. It's one thing for a struggling golfer to feel down and disappointed in response to poor play. This is normal and to be expected. It's quite another matter when the disappointment lasts for hours or even days, or for the feelings to incorporate issues that pertain to basic self-worth. Golfers who get down to this extent need to carefully examine what composes their thoughts when they are depressed. The technique of cognitive restructuring could then be applied for the purpose of changing these distorted patterns of thinking.

The story of Dan illustrates the effective restructuring of irrational cognitions. A 23-year-old man who was hopeful of gaining eligibility for an assistant pro's card, Dan was referred to me by his physician for depression. Dan had a fabulous high-school golf career, during which time he captained his school team and twice qualified for the state finals. He got some national attention and three Division I schools expressed an interest in him. Unfortunately, his father had died when Dan was 10, and his mother and two younger sisters needed him to bring home a paycheck. His dream was to be able to provide his family with financial support while at the same time remaining involved in the game he loved so deeply, the game that his father first exposed him to at the age of 4. If he could get his professional eligibility, he would be in a position to realize this dream.

While working in a retail position, Dan kept up his golf skills, working on all phases of his game seven days a week. The day before a 36-hole qualifying event, he shot a practice round of 69. He was confident going into the qualifiers, knowing that an average of 75 would be good enough to launch him on a career as a golf professional. Unfortunately, Dan's putter failed him in the early phases of the critical round and he never recovered. When he failed to qualify, he was utterly demoralized, left with no hope for realizing his career goals. In the three weeks that followed this devastating disappointment, Dan lost ten pounds and was sleeping excessively.

The fact that I was a psychologist who was also a golf fanatic provided Dan with the comfort he needed to open right up. His depression, as he interpreted it, was because he was a failure who never came through when the pressure was on. "Why shouldn't I be depressed," he explained. "I'm a loser."

Before Dan could be ready to restructure distorted cognitions about himself, he needed to develop some degree of insight into the origins of his twisted thought patterns. Most significantly, he needed to recognize the extent to which he tied his successful golf performance to a feeling of being secure in his father's love. Dan's greatest memories of his childhood were based on the pride his father displayed about his golf potential. When his father died, the portion of Dan's identity development which depended on the positive identification with his father was incomplete. He still needed his father to serve as a role model, to instill in him feelings of worthiness and pride. Dan's premature loss of his father was traumatic for him. And golf remained the only connection he had to his dad. The only manner in which he could feel that he measured up.

Once he became equipped with some insight, Dan was able to challenge his cognitive distortions with contrary evidence. He came to recognize that if he was really a loser, he wouldn't have won match after match as a high-school student. He wouldn't have made it to the state finals, and three Division I schools would not have considered investing in his potential for solid play. Dan came to realize that he had one bad event. Granted, it was the most important competitive event of his life, but it still was one single competition in his life. There had been other rounds on different days, and there would be more opportunities in the future. Today, Dan is a successful assistant pro at a prominent club. He continues to work hard and believes in his chances to eventually secure a position as a head professional. One younger sister just graduated with honors from a top-notch college and another is in the midst of her sophomore year. Dan has been instrumental in financially and emotionally supporting them both. This accomplishment has left him feeling proud of himself and comforted by the awareness that his father would be proud as well.

Dan had to work hard to reprogram the way he thought and felt about his golf performance and about himself. He had to unravel antiquated, negative thoughts that automatically ran through his mind. To do this, he first had to do some honest soul-searching, and then go about the business of restructuring these distorted cognitions. Insight alone will not do it. Old thoughts become automatic thoughts that will continue to replay unless time and proper technique are invested in changing them.

Many of the techniques that worked for Dan, and that can work for you as well, are detailed in the book *Feeling Good* by David Burns. Dr. Burns is a cognitive therapist who has had extensive research and clinical experience in the area of altering automatic and self-critical thoughts. He has identified ten different types of cognitive distortions that depressed individuals typically engage in. Two of these, all-or-nothing and overgeneralized thinking, are particularly applicable to Hazard Three golfers.

All-or-Nothing Thinking

THIS TYPE OF DISTORTED THINKING IS ALSO SOMETIMES REFERRED to as black-and-white or dichotomous thinking. It pertains to the tendency to see a less than ideal performance as representing total failure. There is no in-between, shades of gray for all-or-nothing thinkers. I recall, after horribly inept rounds, that my depressed feelings were accompanied by the thought that I was simply a horrible athlete who was kidding himself about ever being a decent golfer. In reality, the truth was that although I may not have been a great athlete, I was not all that bad. The issue was not black or white, all or nothing. By looking around me—at all the poorer athletes who were far better golfers than myself—I began to establish a body of evidence that was contrary to my irrational beliefs. Over time, my harshly self-critical thoughts began to be rivaled by a gentler and fairer voice. At first, the depressed feelings continued despite the more positive thought patterns. But as thunder always follows lightning, emotional change typically arrives after intellectual or cognitive patterns have been altered. Once the thoughts began to change, the process was well under way, and the feelings eventually came around as well.

Overgeneralization

GOLFERS WHO OVERGENERALIZE WILL VIEW A *SINGLE* NEGATIVE experience as representing an overall pattern that is also negative. These individuals are bound to the emotion they are experiencing in the present moment and unfortunately believe it to be true of their life in general. When Dan performed poorly in his qualifying round, he overgeneralized his performance on that particular day to his entire life. The depression and self-disdain he experienced in response to this experience became, to his way of thinking, the way his life was and always would be. Any Hazard Three golfer who remains depressed for days or even hours after a poor golf outing is guilty of overgeneralized and distorted reasoning. To feel extreme despair in response to substandard play, and especially to bring it home and take it out on family and friends, is a pretty sick scenario. The golfer suffers and relationships are strained. And for what? Better to come to terms with the source of this craziness, restructure those irrational, self-critical thoughts and, in the process, start playing a smarter, better, and certainly more enjoyable brand of golf.

The Pathway to a New Style of Thinking

SELF-DESTRUCTIVE THOUGHTS THAT ARE DEEPLY PROGRAMMED DO not change overnight. What is required to replace these old and automatic thought patterns is repetition. For most individuals, it is difficult to consistently maintain the discipline to be able to impose positive self-statements—particularly during moments of sadness and despair. For this reason, Hazard Three's need a plan to help them not buy into the self-deprecating lies that so often follow poor golf performance.

After a disappointing golf round, divide a sheet into two columns. In the left-hand column, make a list of the self-critical thoughts you are experiencing. Then in the right-hand column, write down a rational defense for each of the statements on the left. The two-column list might look something like the following:

SELF-CRITICISM	SELF-DEFENSE
I'm a rotten golfer.	I had a bad day. I've played better before and will do so again in the future.
I don't do anything well.	I cannot judge my entire life on the basis of my golf performance. I have a good job and family along with a couple of good friends.
I feel so depressed. So empty inside.	Feelings are not what my life's about. Within a matter of hours or even moments, I will feel entirely differently.

By making a list, you will be laying out, in black and white, the manner in which your feelings and thoughts become entangled to the point where they make you miserable. Just reading the two columns of statements will help you see how lost you can become in irrational thinking patterns. If your goal is to overcome Hazard Three tendencies, get into the habit of routinely making a list of postround thoughts. And make sure to read them on a regular basis, especially *before* a golf outing. In a short while you will notice a substantial shift in the way you respond to poor play.

The self-hypnotic technique elaborated in Chapter 3 is another excellent method to help facilitate the reprogramming of cognitive distortions. In and of themselves, the techniques of breathing and progressive relaxation are not that useful for the more cognitive, less physiological tendency of the Hazard Three golfer to get too up or too down. However, when these methods are employed while listening to a prerecorded, positive self-statement, it is a very powerful way to access subconscious thought patterns. The Hazard Three golfer who admits that golf-related mood swings are a part of a more basic problem of low self-esteem will be ready to reprogram thinking with a new supply of "mind tapes." Self-hypnosis will greatly facilitate this reprogramming effort. Your mind will become equipped with a set of new tapes that will, in time, automatically play back in your head. The new message will warn you to avoid getting too up or too down and that you are more than your golf game. You will be reminded that everyone has good days and bad days—and if you keep your emotions on an even keel, today could very well be your day.

One Shot at a Time

DURING HIS TWENTY-FIRST YEAR AS A PROFESSIONAL, AT THE AGE of 43, historically struggling to break into the ranks of the top 50 PGA golfers, Mark McCumber had an amazing year in 1994. With seven Tour wins, he finished third on the money list, behind only Nick Price and Greg Norman. Why the sudden turnaround? McCumber offered the following explanation: "All year, I concentrated on 'Forget the last shot.' It takes so long to accept that you can't always replicate your swing. The only thing that you can control is your attitude toward the next shot."

Mark McCumber stumbled upon a simple reality that Zen Bhuddists have known about for thousands of years. That there exists only one moment. That regardless of how fleeting and intangible it is, that moment is now. Whether you are tying a shoe, eating a slice of pizza, looking through a briefcase, or talking on the telephone, there always exists a very specific, always changing moment that is uniquely now. Everyone who is not a Zen master struggles with this concept, but Hazard Threes experience particular difficulty with living in the present moment.

"If I par the last three holes, I'll have my all-time best round." *"If I didn't get that triple bogey on seven, I could have broken ninety."* Sound familiar? If you find yourself thinking about past or future holes or rounds, if you find yourself thinking about anything other than the shot you are currently facing, you are adding needless strokes to your game. Good golfers know to focus on *process* rather than *product*. They operate on a faith that if they put all their energy into the process of one "shot at a time" golf, the score or product will reflect this focus. Successful businessmen employ the same ideology. Rather than focus on bottom-line income, they invest in the process of building good

relationships and being trustworthy and reliable. They know that the money will be there as a by-product of the accumulation of thousands of intelligently lived moments.

And so it goes with golf. If you're a Hazard Three golfer, you probably look at the scorecard too often, and rarely invest yourself in the shot at hand. It might not be an easy task, but work on learning to let go of the horrible shot, or for that matter, of the spectacular shot you hit on some prior hole. It's over and done with, embedded in the forever lost files of spent moments. Also, fight your tendency to anticipate a hole you have yet to play, one that always gives you trouble, or that you might have birdied the last time out. Thinking about it will not help prepare you for it when you get there. What it will do is remove your focus from the task at hand.

Wherever you are, whatever you're thinking or feeling, however good or poorly you're playing, take the time to look around you and experience the moment. Look at the sky, smell the pine, feel the grass beneath your feet as you walk up the fairway. Feel your lungs expand as you breathe deeply, feel your body as you stretch your neck, arms, back, and shoulders. This is a wonderful moment, and you're doing what you most enjoy. You're alive and well, not a care in the world. Next, see your ball and begin to study the shot you're about to hit. Think only of your lie, the wind, yardage, pin placement, and club selection. Imagine the feel of a smooth and fluid swing. See yourself making that swing. If for only a moment you feel the tug of distraction and your mind begins to drift, think of Mark McCumber. And think about the exciting payoff that's the reward for living in the present moment and focusing on the shot at hand.

Be Proactive

As a Hazard Three golfer, you tend to play the role of the victim. If you cannot blame the wind, slow play, or an ill-placed sprinkler head for poor play, you will retreat into a dispirited, helpless, hopeless funk. Believing that you are simply a loser, you feel powerless to do anything for yourself. This passive, reactive state of mind is exactly the opposite way that successful people think and feel. In his best-seller, *The Seven Habits of Highly*

Effective People, author Stephen R. Covey emphasizes the importance of being *proactive,* or taking responsibility for your own life.
He points out that the word *responsibility*—"response-ability"—
literally means the ability to choose your response. He goes on to
state that "Highly proactive people recognize that responsibility.
They do not blame circumstances, conditions, or conditioning for
their behavior. Their behavior is a product of their own conscious
choice, based on values, rather than a product of their conditions,
based on feeling."

The first step in overcoming destructive mood swings on the
golf course, and in life, is to take more responsibility for these
feelings. By being more proactive, you can *take charge* of a situation by developing a plan and remaining committed to it. The
benefits of proactivity are well illustrated by the case of Susan. I
met Susan after a golf psychology seminar I had just presented
at a golf school. Waiting until the room had cleared, Susan, an
athletic-looking woman who appeared to be in her early thirties,
nervously approached me and gave me the following account:

> *I probably need a psychologist more than a swing instructor be-
> cause I'm totally psyched out about my game. I'm in the worst slump
> of my life. I can't hit the ball at all. My teacher today told me that
> my swing was fine, and after I calmed down, I did manage to hit a
> few good shots at the practice range. But after instruction, when I
> went out for nine holes, I was totally lost again. After I missed my
> driver on the first hole, I used my three-wood on two. By the seventh
> hole, I was teeing off with my five-iron. And I couldn't even hit that!
> I have always depended on my fairway woods, but I couldn't possibly
> even consider attempting that now. Golf is such an important part
> of my life. It's always been my way of getting away from stress.
> Now, I'm so depressed after I play, that I actually am relieved when
> the weekends are over, so I can get away from the game and get back
> to work.*

Susan appeared to me as a rather intense and neurotic woman,
who probably struggled with several of Golf's Mental Hazards.
But Hazard Three was clearly evident on the basis of her help-
lessly depressed response to her poor play, and by the degree to
which she invested her ego in her quality of play. Recognizing

that I could not begin to solve all of this woman's problems at this point (the cocktail party began in fifteen minutes), I offered her a very structured plan that was based on the principle of proactivity. She appeared relieved to have some plan, any plan, and agreed to give it a whirl when she was on the course the following afternoon.

I explained to Susan that she was overwhelmed by a multitude of thoughts about mechanics and club selection. Beyond these golf-related concerns, she also was burdened by the psychological questions about her ability and whether she would ever come out of this miserable slump. I advised her to keep it simple and give her mind a break. I agreed to tell her how to approach the nine holes she would play on the following day and even went so far as to tell her what to think about. After reviewing her repertoire of swing thoughts, we settled on "left shoulder under the chin at the top of the backswing" as the only thought she would use during tomorrow's round. She would tee off on every driving hole with her 3-wood, and would use this same club off the fairway as well. She agreed that these rules could not vary, and even if she was playing horribly, she must commit to the plan regarding club selection and the use of a single swing thought for the entire nine holes. One final agreed-upon condition was that she would not practice at all before this round. The next time Susan would swing a golf club would be the following afternoon with her 3-wood on the first tee. I told her I would be curious to know how she did and would look for her on the putting green after her round was complete.

I was practicing five-footers when I saw her. From a distance, I could see a look of contained joy on Susan's face. As she got closer, she broke into a full smile. "It worked," she said. "I didn't score real well, but I struck the ball nicely, better than I have in a long time."

"What worked?" I asked, my tongue scraping the side of my cheek.

"Sticking with the plan you gave me," she responded.

"Why do you think the plan I gave you worked?" I asked as I pulled a five-foot putt 15 inches to the left of the hole.

She look puzzled, as if the question had an obvious answer. "Because I stopped thinking so much?"

Having missed my fourth consecutive putt, I laid my putter down and responded. "It was more than that, Susan. Sure, it was good that you stopped thinking so much, but more important, you took charge of the situation. You had a plan and stuck with it. For the first time in a while, *you* were in control."

"Not really," she countered. "*You* gave me the plan. *You* told me what I should focus on."

I love a power trip as much as the next guy, but fair is fair. "I'd love to take the credit for your good play today, but think about what really happened out there. I don't know you and I've never seen you swing a golf club. All I did was randomly pick a swing thought for you and randomly tell you what clubs to hit. What I did do was to temporarily take the responsibility of decision-making off your shoulders. You became so down on yourself that you lost all self-trust. It was easier for you to trust me than to trust yourself."

"But how can I learn to trust myself?" she asked.

"By taking responsibility for your performance," I replied. "If you're faltering, pick a plan, any plan, and stick to it. I don't care if you go out with only a five-iron and a putter. If you don't know what to do, don't wait around for some answer to descend from the heavens. Make a plan and write it down. Then stick with it. Today you made a commitment to me, next time make a commitment to yourself. Even if it doesn't go as well as it went today, you will know that you had a plan and that you were not rolling over and playing dead. You'll know that you were still in charge of your life."

Susan walked away feeling—for the moment at least—hopefully proactive and I went back to my putting practice. I missed six out of six five-footers. Then four out of five from even closer range. I was all out of sync, beginning to get uptight about the round I had scheduled for the following morning with a couple of the teaching pros at the school. Should I switch back to the other putter I had in my trunk? Maybe it was time to go back to the reverse overlap grip. Keep it simple, I thought. Bring the putter back slowly, keep my head down until I hear the sound of the ball dropping in the cup. I managed to knock a few down and got out of there while the going was good.

Disappointment as Opportunity

I HAVE HEARD THAT THE CHINESE SYMBOL FOR CRISIS IS THE SAME as the symbol for opportunity. As a Hazard Three golfer, you could probably derive a great deal of benefit from an understanding of the wisdom inherent in this linguistic oddity. When you experience disappointment on the golf course, you are too deeply ingrained in feelings of dejection and low self-worth to recognize the opportunity for learning and growth that is right in front of your face.

Dr. J. Mitchell Perry is the founder of Perry Performance Classics, a seminar company that focuses on the similarities between success in the business world and success on the golf course. He talks about "Recovery Mode," or the inevitability of having to learn to recover from disappointment both in business *and* in golf. In an interview with *Golf* magazine, Perry suggested that you "Notice your reaction to a missed shot or a lost sale. Good recovery is tough if you tell yourself you've failed. Don't trash yourself. Train yourself to immediately concentrate on what you'll do differently to improve your results next time."

Rather than dwell on the negative feelings that result from the disappointment of poor play, is there anything that can be learned from the experience? I remember a particular match that occurred during my first season as a league player that taught me a valuable lesson in converting disappointment into opportunity. I was playing against the defending Flight A champion. Even though I was getting 6 strokes for 9 holes, I didn't really expect very much from myself against an obviously seasoned pressure player. My expectations, however, were significantly altered after the second-handicap, first hole. I pulled my approach to the par four well left, and he was comfortably on, 12 feet away in two. Even though I was getting a stroke for the hole, I took a disinterested whack for my third shot, but still managed to get it on the green, about 40 feet from the pin. First to putt, I didn't pay much attention to break and attempted to get the speed about right. I gave it a roll, watched the ball wobble and strain, break a foot left during the last 8 feet of roll, and run out of gas just as it fell into the hole.

When my opponent lipped out his birdie putt, my par won

the hole. First off the tee on two, the reigning league champion
pushed his drive over the net that contained the driving range
and teed up another, now hitting 3. I parred the hole to go 2 up.
The unexpected pattern continued for five holes, three of which
I won, with the remaining two holes halved. On the tee at 6, my
good-sport opponent took the scorecard out of his back pocket,
studied it, and reported that he hadn't won a single hole to that
point and would have to win all four remaining holes to pull
out the match. I also recall some comments on the subject of
sandbagging that were being tossed around.

After I played the last four holes in ten over, I felt that I had
earned the right to declare myself a choker. Afterward in the
clubhouse, I made light of my demise, sloughing it off to inex-
perience and to a formidable opponent. I played the classy,
humble-in-defeat loser role quite well. The walls didn't come
crashing down until early the next morning, when I awoke to
replay what had happened in my mind. Hole by hole, I thought
about every shot, every lost opportunity. As many times as I
played it over, I could not change the outcome. And I could not
rid myself of a sick, almost nauseated feeling of ineptitude and
regret.

A couple of days after "black Wednesday," I decided to call
Tom, my personal golf swing guru and lifter of spirits. On the
practice tee, during my lesson, we talked very little about my
swing mechanics. Rather, in response to my disappointment,
Tom said things like, "We've all been there," and "You've got to
blow some of those chances, so when they happen again, you'll
be ready." When the lesson was completed, Tom had accomplished two things. First, he convinced me to spend more time
on my chipping, which was the reason I lost at least two of the
latter holes of the match. His second accomplishment was to
convince me that I should actually be relieved to have had this
negative experience, that is was a necessary rite of passage that
all golfers need to experience sooner or later. My golf pro turned
the psychological tables on me and had me believing that I'd be
ready the next time out.

My test came five weeks later. Fast out of the gate again, I was
up 4–1 after five holes. Getting ready to hit off the 6th tee, no
one had to draw me a picture. The match became a dogfight,

with my opponent playing great scrambling golf to win the next two holes. I felt good about the fact that I, too, was playing well and was not giving away the match as I had done five weeks previously. But still, I had an uneasy sense of déja vu as I stood ready to hit on the par-three, 160-yard, 8th hole. These short holes were typically easy for me. I generally hit my middle-irons straight, and always got them airborne. But not this time. A topped line drive, center of the fairway, about 30 yards short of the green. My opponent had already hit, and was looking at a 15-foot birdie opportunity.

I took my time walking to my ball and reflected on the situation. There were no strokes awarded for this hole, my opponent would certainly two-putt for par, and I needed a tough up-and-down to maintain my one hole advantage. If I lost this hole, the match would be all square going into the par-five 9th. My opponent was a big hitter who relished the par fives, particularly those like the wide-open 9th, which would, if necessary, accommodate his occasional severe slice. I knew that losing this match would be a tough pill for me. I was determined to not give it away.

I don't remember grabbing my sand wedge, don't remember anything beyond that point. To this day I am still amazed at how close that ball came to going into the hole. My chip landed softly on the green, rolled like a putt, rimmed the cup before settling an inch away. I still remember the look on my opponent's face, and how I watched *him* be the one to quit on himself as he three-putted for bogey. Even though the match was over, I won the 9th with a par. My opponent took a triple bogey.

Disappointment as opportunity? You bet. It's true in golf, it's true in business, and it's true in life. I feel obliged to give myself credit for turning my disappointing experience into an opportunity. I might have been down after blowing that first match, but rather than sulk in self-pity, I sought out advice from a professional that I trusted. And just as important, I followed his advice. When I think back on it all, I am still amazed that the critical shot in the second match was the very type of chip shot that Tom suggested I practice. And somehow, I don't see it as coincidence. After all, golf is an amazing game that reflects this amazing life. It is a life that can baffle and oftentimes be cruel and seemingly unjust. Yet, somehow I believe that there is a pattern to it all that is fair and makes perfect sense. That there are principles and formulas that work without fail. It's just a matter of figuring out and then following the rules of the game. The Chinese seem to have caught on a long time ago.

6

HAZARD FOUR:
Worrying What Others Think

"Man is the only animal that blushes. Or needs to."

—MARK TWAIN

Kathy felt all eyes upon her, as she stood over her ball, about to tee off on the first hole. Gazing down at the white sphere suspended a half-inch above the rich green carpet that covered the tee area, she felt outside of herself.

Oh, God, Kathy thought, this is starting to feel just like the first tee at Tidewater. On that particular outing, with husband and best friends watching, Kathy had hit under the ball, knocking the tee ahead ten yards, and leaving the ball cradled comfortably in the divot left by her driver.

She tried to refocus but still felt all eyes, most notably her own, watching and waiting. They were standing in judgment, ready to evaluate her athletic ability and mental fortitude. She saw herself, her broad rear in those unflattering yellow culottes, shuffling her feet, struggling to find a comfortable position. See the ball, she told herself. She brought the club back, praying that her body would somehow remember. She just wanted it to be over, so that she could escape from the fixed gazes that stood ready to offer approval or to quietly turn away.

Standing on the tee is a lonely place for any golfer. It is an especially lonely place for a Hazard Four golfer such as Kathy.

Good golf requires a clear, worry-free mind, and a relaxed body. How could Kathy, with her preoccupation about performance and prior failure, possibly be in a position to rhythmically swing a golf club and make clean and square contact with the ball? The chances were indeed very slim. The steady stream of isolated, "center-stage" moments that constitute a central part of the golfing ritual leaves the self-conscious Hazard Four golfer at high-risk for a self-destructive performance.

Hazard Four Characteristics

NOT UNLIKE GOLFERS WHO STRUGGLE WITH HAZARD ONE, HAZard Four golfers also experience a good deal of anxiety. But it is a totally different type. You will recall that the Hazard One golfer experienced a free-floating, "fear of fear" brand of anxiety that could not be attributed to anything in particular. Hazard Fours, on the other hand, know exactly why they feel the way they do, since their anxiety is a social one, centering on the worry that others will not think well of them.

Tees and greens are the settings for most Hazard Four problems. Because both of these areas promote congregation of the golf group, the Hazard Four golfer feels more closely scrutinized. The hacker is typically most anxious on the tee (particularly the first tee). Low handicappers and professional golfers, on the other hand, have trust in their ability to consistently drive the ball. For them, the green is the most common setting for the embarrassing moment.

The number-one mental affliction of the professional golfer is the dreaded yip. From Ben Hogan to Johnny Miller, and more recently Tom Watson, the short putt is far more frightening than a drive onto a narrow fairway or an approach over 150 yards of water. Not only does a short putt appear to be an easy opportunity, but the putt is the final stroke that closes out a hole. A tee shot that misses the fairway, or an approach that lands in a trap, can be compensated for on the next shot. The missed short and "easy" putt counts as a stroke—as significant to the final score as a 280-yard drive—that cannot be recovered. And to miss a short, seemingly easy putt in front of co-players, a gallery, and a television audience is a dreaded moment of embarrassment for the professional golfer. Sam Snead was quoted as saying, "I shot a wild elephant in Africa thirty yards from me, and it didn't hit the ground until it was right at my feet. I wasn't a bit scared, but a four-foot putt scares me to death."

Whereas, Hazard Three golfers become dreadfully down on *themselves* in response to substandard play, Hazard Four golfers believe that *others* are down on them during periods of ineptness. I recall a round where I played for the first time with the son of my secretary. A big, strapping, athletic young man, he had a smooth and powerful swing that he never got going that day. His big drives went straight out for about 200 yards, before turning left, and covering another 100 yards, into the depths of Marlboro Country. Despite his erratic play, he remained even-tempered, and the rest of us enjoyed his company. In the parking lot, saying our goodbyes, I was surprised when he "apologized for not playing very well." He acted as if he thought that I was disappointed in him. In truth, I was too preoccupied with my own game to give his level of play any second thought.

The level of play for the recreational golfer who struggles with Hazard Four is also influenced by playing partners. Because of their hyperawareness of other golfers' perceptions, Hazard Four golfers are more comfortable playing with individuals they regard as being unthreatening. This determination is usually made on the basis of skill level and/or personality. I know that when I first began to play, most of my golfing friends had been at the game for years, and were capable of shooting scores in the 80s. My first time ever, triple-bogey round from hell would have been much easier if I had gone out with players who were closer to my ability level (not easy to find). But my friends were kind and supportive and seemed to even get a kick out of watching me suffer. In the end, I believe that playing with better players set my standards higher and helped me progress more rapidly than if I had started out with other beginners.

If your score for Hazard Four on the *MHAS* was elevated, you struggle with at least some of the socially oriented, interpersonal problems that are inherent in the game of golf. You very likely also struggle with an inferiority complex. In order to feel a sense of satisfaction with your game, you require that others are impressed with your level of play. Because you tend to be down on yourself much of the time, you cannot rely on your own feelings and thoughts to provide you with a sense of well-being and competence. Along these lines, Hazard Four shares the relevance of self-esteem issues that were discussed in reference to Hazards Two and Three. And as was the case with these other hazards, the problems that pertain to low self-esteem apply not just on the golf course but in other areas of your life as well.

Kathy's concern with her performance on the first tee was indicative of a level of self-consciousness that no doubt extended beyond the golf course. Her concern about her playing partners' reaction to her performance was rooted in her low self-esteem. Her perception of others' feelings toward her controlled her level of positive self-worth. This method of self-judgment inevitably leads to conclusions that are unfair, irrational, and self-destructive.

Kathy's feelings of inferiority and low self-worth go beyond simple issues of vanity and are rooted deep within her psyche. If you also worry about the reaction of others to the manner in which you hit a golf ball, or about other socially embarrassing situations—perhaps making a conversational blunder in front of an employer, or appearing foolish in a social situation—you also need to delve into this distorted method for determining self-worth. Investing in the process of overcoming the fear of what others think of you will serve you well, not just on the golf course, but in other areas of your life as well.

All of the techniques that were discussed previously—breathing, relaxation, cognitive restructuring, and self-hypnosis—are applicable for the management of Hazard Four. Breathing and relaxation can help reduce the physiological symptoms of anxiety which are part and parcel of the social anxiety experienced by Hazard Four individuals. Research has indicated that self-conscious individuals, who are accustomed to "turning inward," will find the practice of meditation or relaxation relatively easy to engage in. The Hazard Four's introspective nature will likewise be advantageous for developing the insight necessary to restructure the irrational thinking patterns that typically accompany the problem of low self-esteem. Along these lines, the techniques of cognitive restructuring and self-hypnosis will benefit the Hazard Four individual. The following sections of this chapter will specifically address the nature of these distorted and unhealthy cognitions and will provide models for improved patterns of thinking.

The Shame-Based Identity

ENVISION THE YOUNG CHILD WHO GETS CAUGHT WITH "A HAND IN the cookie jar" or the older child who is publicly ridiculed by a teacher. The reaction is typically a red-faced, head-hanging look of deep and utter shame. This shameful response to an embarrassing moment, much like the "fight-or-flight" response, is an innate and necessary reaction. The fact that we recognize and feel bad about having broken a societal rule leads to the development of a conscience and enables some semblance of law and order.

As is true with all normal and healthy emotions, the experience of shame could be excessive. Do you lie in bed replaying conversations, thinking about how stupid or ridiculous you probably sounded? Can you be given multiple forms of praise for a project or work assignment, and be also offered a single instance of criticism, and remain down and totally fixed upon the one critical point? If your response to these questions is affirmative, the manner in which you experience shame is excessive and unhealthy. Current-day psychological jargon would describe you as having a shame-based identity. This means that a good deal of the time, you see yourself as a flawed, even worthless individual. That you are only entitled to feel good about yourself on the basis of someone else's positive perspective of your worthiness.

An important part of the identity of healthy individuals is based on feeling connected to others, on not feeling separate and alone. As a Hazard Four golfer, this portion of your identity is incomplete and seeks connectedness on the basis of others' being impressed with your golf game. When you play well, you feel self-assured, one of the gang. On those days when your game is off, you experience the isolating emotion of shame, which immediately cuts the ties that connect you to the rest of the world. You are doomed to feelings of pain and alienation.

Did your parents often tell you that, *"You should be ashamed of yourself!"* If your family was like most families, it's very likely that they did. Shame is an extremely powerful emotion in that the manner in which you experienced it as a child could potentially stay with you throughout your entire life. What changes is that as an adult, you have internalized the harsh, critical voice of your parent(s). It is now *you* shouting and continually reminding yourself that *"You deserve to be ashamed!"*

As a Hazard Four golfer with a shame-based identity, you dread the embarrassment that goes with poor play. Flub a drive, miss a two-foot putt, and you hear the voice of the critical parent that resides within you reminding you of the scornful judgments of those around you. You feel ashamed and unworthy. But stop for a moment to consider the fact that you are no longer a child and that you do have the power to change your thinking patterns, to formulate your own self-evaluations. Along with the automatic and critical thoughts that unconsciously spring from your "child's" brain is a mature, adult brain that could step back and reevaluate the evidence. The conscious brain of the adult knows that it is unfair to judge your self-worth solely on the basis of golf performance. That even if you are justified for feeling somewhat down about missed opportunities on the golf course, it is still ridiculous to feel a level of embarrassment and shame that embodies your entire spirit. Suppose you brought your 8-year-old son, nephew, or neighbor out on the course for the purpose of exposing him to the game. You would probably make every effort to be supportive and positive. If you were critical and negative, you know that this kid would have no chance of performing well or, for that matter, of ever enjoying the game. You would no doubt look for positive instances that would provide the opportunity to be encouraging. If, for instance, the kid took ten swipes at the ball before reaching the green on a short par three, missed two putts, and then sank a three-footer for a 13, you would probably respond by saying, "Nice putt. That was a good, smooth stroke." Why should you deny yourself that same consideration and support?

The Imaginary Audience

EVERY RECREATIONAL GOLFER WHO HAS EVER SEEN A PRO TOURNAment in person or watched one on television has asked the same two questions: (1) How can these guys perform with hundreds of people standing all around them and millions more watching on television? (2) How the heck can these players hit the ball into the narrow tunnel that is created by a gallery-lined fairway, and not worry about killing someone? The second question was answered for all the hackers of the world by ex-president Gerald Ford, who figured that anyone in the gallery at a Pro-Am either had a death wish or was willing to risk their life for a glimpse of the action. The answer to the first question has to do with the professional golfer's level of confidence as well as with their very special ability to literally block out the world and to focus on the task at hand.

As a Hazard Four golfer, you do just the opposite of this. Playing golf in the private, expansive domain of your home course—no cameraman, television wires, autograph seekers, interview requests—with just a few familiar faces around, you play each shot as if the world was watching you protect a one-shot lead in the final round at Augusta. You feel your every movement being carefully watched and judged. Might as well bring out the gallery and TV cameras. At least then, your self-conscious concerns would be somewhat justified.

Psychologists have long recognized adolescence as a stage of life that is encumbered by egocentrism, preoccupation with appearance, and self-conscious concerns about what other people think. The term "imaginary audience" was coined to describe the adolescent's perspective of always feeling watched and scrutinized. This notion was made very clear to me several years ago while I served as a chaperone at a middle-school dance. I sat at a table by the entrance to the gymnasium where the dance was being held. I watched the young girls fixing their hair, adjusting their clothes, frightfully making their entrance into the gym. They all acted like queens entering the grand ballroom, where the eyes of all their subjects would be upon them. And the boys were not that much better. I recall one awkward, blemished 13-year-old male who fought with his mother and finally refused to enter at all. The problem? He had a pea-sized food stain on the front of his shirt.

Everyone normally maintains some degree of egocentrism beyond adolescence and throughout life. Show a set of photographs or a video to a room full of supposedly mature grown-ups, and I guarantee all you will hear will be a series of comments along the lines of "*I* look so fat," "Does *my* voice really sound like that?" "That jacket looks horrible on *me!*" The reality is that we have been sentenced to an entire life of living exclusively in one body, and watching the world through the same set of eyes. It is no wonder that, to a great extent, we *are* self-absorbed. It all comes down to the degree to which we practice our egocentrism. Truly mature adults know that people are people, and no one is all that unique. They also recognize that people are too preoccupied with their *own* concerns about how others see *them* to be concerned about the appearance or behavior of anyone else.

When I watch golfers standing around the first tee, I am reminded of those middle-school kids. Each individual is so immersed in his or her own performance outcome, and so concerned with avoiding the embarrassment of not getting off the tee in a respectable fashion. That's why the first tee is the place to get all excuses out in the open. "I haven't even been to the range for two weeks." "I've been sick all week, I don't expect to play very well." "I've had this sore right shoulder that's really killing me now. I probably shouldn't even be playing." There might not be a gallery or television audience out there, but Hazard Four golfers feel the pressure to perform and avoid embarrassment. Like Kathy, at the top of this chapter, who felt "everyone" gazing in judgment at her, she was in reality performing to an audience of one.

Nobody Cares

IF THERE IS ANY PLACE ON THIS PLANET WHERE PEOPLE ARE SELF-absorbed, it's on the golf course. Do you really care if your partner is playing poorly if *you* are having the round of your life? Hell no! Sure, it's more fun when everyone plays well. You're happy, and the company is a lot more pleasant. But if you had to pick one member of your foursome to be on their game, who would it be? Face it, unless you've paid a pro for a playing lesson, no one cares about *your* swing, no one is assessing *your* ability to handle pressure situations, and nobody cares about *your* score (assuming all bets are off).

I once worked with a young poet who struggled with performance anxiety in a manner that reminded me of the plight of the Hazard Four golfer. Mitch was a 25-year-old doctoral student who was asked to read a few of his poems at a university-sponsored gathering which would feature several young area poets. I had read Mitch's work, thought it was quite good, and encouraged him to participate. Flattered by the invitation and by my support, Mitch agreed to do it. As the date drew closer, Mitch's anxiety continued to increase, until he considered finding a graceful way to bow out of the proceedings. Mitch was nervous about performing in front of a group of people, but this concern was secondary to his fear of being judged by his peers. He explained:

> *These poets are good. They've all read numerous times before. They're going to think my poems are stupid, maybe even infantile. Wait until they hear the one that describes old age as a return to infancy. It's so corny. I hate that poem! There's so much they could pick apart. These people are serious poets. I'm telling you, they're going to laugh at me. Why should I put myself in a situation that's going to destroy my spirit? I had to be crazy to have ever accepted the invitation in the first place!*

With cognitive therapy, Mitch and I delved into the rational evidence that contradicted his distorted cognitions. For instance, we considered the fact that the people who sponsored the readings were faculty who not only were competent judges of quality poetry, but also had no doubt read some of Mitch's poems before inviting him. And who was Mitch to determine whether his poems were good or not? Poetry is a very subjective art form, and the poet is probably the last person who can objectively evaluate the merits of his own work. Finally, I convinced Mitch that all the poets would be nervous and would be concerned with one and only one issue on the night of the readings. That is, the response to *their* poetry. Just as Mitch couldn't care less about what the other poets had written, nobody was going to care about the content of his poetry. Aided by self-hypnosis, Mitch mustered up the courage to perform that evening, much to his surprised delight, to a favorable response. He could not help but speculate on the reasons for two of the other poets' last-minute decision to withdraw from the presentation.

Whether you're with a group of poets or the foursome on the first tee, it is important to overcome the self-centered belief that everyone will be watching and judging your performance. Consider how you feel when everyone except one member of your foursome hits a good drive. Assuming you were one of the fortunate golfers, you and the other golfers who found the fairway would not be looking down upon your troubled friend. Why should you? You have all been there and will all be there again. The only thought going through your minds as you watch your despondent friend prepare to recover is, "Thank God it wasn't me."

I close this section by paraphrasing a saying I heard a long time ago. It is a statement about self-consciousness and the aging process and it goes something like this. *When I was twenty, I spent a great deal of time worrying about how others saw me, and what they said about me in my absence. By the time I turned forty, I finally matured to a point where I stopped giving a damn what others had to say about me. When I reached sixty, I came to realize that they weren't talking about me at all.*

Nobody's Perfect

AS IF ON STAGE, PERFORMING TO AN IMAGINARY AUDIENCE, falsely assuming that the members of this "audience" are studying your every move, you feel dissatisfied with anything about yourself that is less than perfect. As a Hazard Four individual, you are excessively self-aware. Much like Kathy, you step "out of yourself" and watch your life as if you were watching a movie. Unfortunately, as a harsh and impossibly demanding critic, who will not be satisfied with anything short of perfection, the reviews are never "two thumbs up."

Linda was a professional model referred to me by a plastic

surgeon. Before agreeing to perform a third nose operation, this surgeon required that she talk to a psychologist and assess her standards as they pertained to her physical appearance. As soon as I saw Linda, I had no problem determining that she was a knockout. When she told me that her nose had "stripes" that formed parentheses around her nostrils, I tried hard to see what she was talking about. On her second visit, she went so far as to bring in a lighted, magnifying mirror, and was shocked when I still could not make out the stripes that were so apparent to her.

When Linda told me that she had fat thighs, the verdict was in. If this woman—all 5 feet 11 inches, 118 pounds of her, who modeled lingerie for a department store—had fat thighs, I made Bhudda look like Woody Allen! All my efforts to contradict Linda's irrational, impossibly perfectionist image of her bodily appearance were met with resistance. Convinced that her problems were physical and not psychological, she left counseling after only a few sessions. If her plastic surgeon refused to perform the surgery on her nose, she remained determined to find another one who would.

How much perfection do you demand from yourself? After a round of golf, do you remember the good moments, or do you dwell on the missed opportunities? I recall playing with a bogey-golfer friend, who had a great day, shooting an 82. Not a big hitter, his drives went about 180 yards and consistently found the fairway all afternoon. His solid fairway wood play and his great putting more than compensated for his lack of distance off the tee. Knowing this friend to be self-critical with perfectionist tendencies, I handed him the money I had lost to him and congratulated him on his great round. Quiet and pensive, he tucked my cash in his wallet and said, "If only I didn't hit those wimpy drives."

Nothing in this life is perfect. As I sit here writing these words, I can't help but wonder if there is not something I'm leaving out, if there is not a better way to express the points I am trying to make. But you know what? It doesn't matter. The words I am stating are the words that are issuing forth from my stream of consciousness. I have no other words available to me. My fingerprints, my golf swing, my thoughts, my mannerisms, all are mine, and there's not a lot I can do to change any of that. If I want to aim for perfectionist ideals, I would never write another word or never swing a golf club again. However, I am fortunate enough to realize that nobody is perfect. And even if I am painfully aware of all the details that comprise my imperfections, I also recognize that no one else will care enough to even notice.

Use a List to Reprogram Thoughts

IF YOU BELIEVE THAT HAZARD FOUR IMPEDES YOUR GOLF GAME, and that you do in fact worry too much about what others think, it is time to reprogram the thoughts that accompany this self-destructive tendency. Cognitive restructuring, a useful method for overcoming the first three hazards, also works well for those who struggle with Hazard Four. On the basis of the contents of previous sections in this chapter, assemble a list similar to the one that was suggested in the previous chapter. In the left-hand column, write down the cognitive distortions that pertain to your Hazard Four destructive thought patterns. Then in the right-hand column, create a second list that consists of rational responses that defend against each of these unfair self-judgments. The following is an example of what such a list might look like:

COGNITIVE DISTORTION	RATIONAL RESPONSE
My swing is ugly, others will be critical of it.	My swing is my swing. I can't change it. No one will be watching it that carefully.
I'll be so embarrassed if I don't get off the first tee.	No one will care if I don't get off the tee. Their only thought will be "better him than me."
I really want my playing partners to be impressed with my game.	They won't care. If I am good company and a courteous golfer, they'll be impressed.

If you are a Hazard Four golfer, take advantage of your bodily self-awareness to practice progressive relaxation, while you expose your mind to your list of truthful and rational self-statements. The resultant technique of self-hypnosis will enable you to reprogram the automatic thoughts that you maintain about being watched and critically judged. Make yourself a tape recording during which you remind yourself that the critical voice that rises from the depths of your subconscious is that of an insensitive "parent" scolding a vulnerable "child" who is deserving of empathy and kindness rather then spirit-breaking put-downs. And remind yourself that within you also exists the voice of a loving parent who can give this child within you what it deserves and needs—a parent who, if given the opportunity, could help you overcome the destructive forces of shame, perfectionism, and self-consciousness. Enough so that you might let up on your tendency toward self-criticism and the worry about other people's opinions about the essence of your character and the quality of your performance. Enough so that you just might become capable of enjoying rather than worrying about the company of your playing partners.

Against the Grain

EMOTIONAL CHANGE ALWAYS LAGS BEHIND INTELLECTUAL IN-sight. Assuming you have successfully reprogrammed your thinking to the point where you appreciate the irrational and ridiculous concerns that go along with being a Hazard Four golfer, you still need to go out and test the waters of this newly found perspective. As was true with the Hazard One problem of anxiety, in order to overcome the Hazard Four problem of self-conscious concern, you must go against the grain of what comes easily and naturally to you. To overcome the self-destructive, hazardous tendency of worrying about what others think, you must go into the teeth of your fear and confront it.

Our self-conscious golfer friend Kathy, who kicked off this chapter, was at least willing to be on that center-stage first tee. The most extreme of Hazard Four golfers are those who dread embarrassment to the point where they never set foot on a golf course at all. Likewise evasive are the talented speakers who avoid public speaking or the talented poets who will not read in front of an audience. Avoiding something that is fearful—so long as it is not a basic activity that is essential to your needs for daily functioning—is not the worse thing in the world. No big deal if you don't play golf or you avoid speaking in public. Life goes on despite these minor avoidances.

But ask yourself the question of how you really feel about living an avoiding life that is controlled by your fears. When you develop insight into the nature of your avoidance of an unpleasant circumstance, and you muster up the courage to confront the situation, your self-esteem soars. Add to this increased positive sense of self-worth the fact that the courage to confront uncomfortable situations will transfer to new and different activities.

You have the power to eventually become an individual who is excited by the prospect of doing things that you were always apprehensive about trying. The possibilities are endless. You can take voice lessons and audition for a part in a musical, you can learn to ice skate or downhill ski, you can write the novel you always dreamed about, you can take a class in line-dancing or even join a golf league. The unpleasant experience of feeling watched and judged might be especially difficult at the beginning. But you also know that the discomfort quickly passes, soon replaced by a sense of pride that is the reward for living a life based on honesty and courage.

7

HAZARD FIVE:
The Need to Be in Control

"God, grant me serenity to accept the
things I cannot change, courage to
change the things I can, and wisdom to
know the difference."

—REINHOLD NIEBUHR

*Everyone at the club referred to him as the "astrophysicist." Lee's
investment in the scientific study of the physics of the golf swing
included a device that recorded clubhead speed, an exercise program
for his left, not his right side, weighted lead tape that he applied to
various portions of the different clubheads in his set, eight different
putters, a metronome he brought with him to the practice range, a
video playback machine that repeated at variable speeds, backward
and forward, mini-fragments of his golf swing, a spandex sleeve that
helped keep his right elbow close to his side, and a lift in his right
golf shoe designed to compensate for his "right-side sag"—a result
of a mild case of scholiosis—that helped him keep the weight inside
his right instep at the top of his backswing.*

*Everyone enjoyed the antics of precise, fastidious, anal, compulsive
Lee. A study in thoroughness and total devotion, he was a well-
respected man. Each afternoon after work, his practice routine was
the same. At the range—clubs placed on the ground in front of him
to enable proper alignment and swing path—he would methodically
go through his routine: fifteen wedges, fifteen 7-irons, fifteen 4-irons,
fifteen drivers. On the putting green just as exacting a pattern: fifty
sand wedges from 25 yards; 75 pitch-and-runs; fifteen each with his*

5- through 9-iron. And finally one hundred putts: twenty each from 30, 20, 10, 5, and 2 feet.

When it came time to play, Lee's preshot routine was just as methodical and exact. After gauging distance, wind conditions, pin placement, and lie, Lee would choose the appropriate club, stand behind his ball, and eye the target. When he stepped up to his shot, it was always left foot first, then the right, grip checked, knees buckled four times, the clubface in line with the target, and finally one picture perfect practice swing. And Lee had the prettiest practice swing at the club. Club parallel to the ground at the top, wrists cocked, right side firing through the hitting zone, finishing with hands high, chest facing the target, all weight resting on the outer edge of his left foot. The routine completed, Lee appeared ready to hit.

But then something happened. Although you could set your watch on the basis of the time it took to perform the precise sequence that preceded this particular moment, when a ball was placed in the way of that mighty swing path, when it came time to bring the club back, the entire process broke down and lost its flow. Lee would lock-in at his address position and stare at the ball for ten seconds, fifteen seconds, maybe longer. Lee, the golfer with the solid fundamentals and impeccable work ethic, was left frozen, straining to pull the trigger during a critical moment of truth that meant so much to him.

Lee was willing to engage in any expense or form of practice that would establish his control over his golf game, but there remained a piece of the puzzle that was missing. Hard work and solid fundamentals are important, but the game of golf extends beyond what is logically apparent into a realm that is more intuitive and mystical. Lee was disconnected from the self-trust and leap of blind faith that are necessary to be a complete golfer. Lee had mastered the golf swing, but he had yet to discover one simple truth: that the only way to gain control is to relinquish control. Lee, the prototypical Hazard Five golfer with his need to be in control, had yet to explore the art of "letting go."

Hazard Five Characteristics

HAVE YOU EVER STOOD FROZEN OVER A GOLF BALL? EVER HAD difficulty bringing the putter back? The example of Lee illustrates a phenomenon that most golfers can appreciate—the phenomenon that occurs during that critical moment of transition when the golfer must break out of the static, contemplative setup and begin the take-away. This moment of truth is one of the things that makes golf such an enormously difficult game. Whereas most sports consist of a series of flowing motions that are based on mindless and instinctual reactions, the golfer must consciously *decide* when the time is right to initiate motion.

When you tackle a runner coming at you or jump for a rebound, there is no time to consider the range of potential outcomes prior to the moment of physical release. When you stand over a golf ball, you can ponder the out-of-bounds region off to the right or the water hazard right in front of you. You can also think about whether or not you will strike the ball cleanly. Because golf is a game that is necessarily composed of many mishits, your memory bank contains all of the beautiful as well as the ugly possibilities. As a Hazard Five golfer standing over your ball, there is time, too much time, to consider the unpredictable outcome of the shot at hand. So you stand there frozen, unable to pull the trigger and "let go" of the control you so desperately want to maintain.

Another reason Hazard Five golfers tend to freeze up over the ball is that they overanalyze their golf swing. Rather than *feel* a whole, fluid golf swing, they attempt to string together all the mechanical *thoughts* that are entailed in a fundamentally correct swing. By so doing, there is the illusion of controlling the path of the golf club and directing the flight of the ball safely out to the landing area. It is for this reason that Hazard Five golfers often have great practice swings that fall apart when a ball is placed in their way. During the practice swing, there is no need for control because there is no result and, therefore, no risk. Place a ball down and suddenly everything is at stake. In an effort to control this unpredictable situation, the Hazard Five golfer abandons the smooth whole *feel* of the practice swing and reverts to the mechanically dissected swing. The result is usually a choppy, whack *at* the ball as opposed to a fluid swing *through* it.

If you scored high for Hazard Five, you probably are a serious student of your swing. You have probably broken it down into a multitude of fragments that are accompanied by an extensive list of swing thoughts—low and slow take-away, wrist cocked, right arm pointing straight up at the top, bring the club from inside to out, delay uncocking wrists until right before impact, throw hands at the target, finish with right shoulder under chin, weight on the front foot. Attempting to process all these thoughts and execute all the proper mechanics during the actual golf swing is impossible, but it gives Hazard Five golfers the delusional feeling of control.

In the introduction to *Golf, the Greatest Game*, John Updike likened the golf swing to "a suitcase into which we are trying to pack one too many items—if we remember to keep our heads still, we forget to shift our weight; if we remember to shift our weight, we lift our head, or stiffen the left knee, or uncock the wrists too soon." And here lies the reason that Hazard Five golfers such as Lee are so likely to freeze up over the ball. The mind becomes overloaded with detail, the "suitcase is too full to be closed." Devoid of intuitive self-trust, the Hazard Five golfer cannot muster up the faith necessary to simply allow the golf swing to happen.

The overanalytical, controlled nature of Hazard Five individuals carries beyond the golf course. In the course of your daily life, you are more comfortable with planned activities rather than spontaneous experience. You possess a "show-me" perspective that requires logical reasoning as opposed to gut-level instincts. You also do not care much for surprises. You prefer your life to be planned and plotted, leaving little room for spontaneity. If you plan a trip to Europe, it will be a prearranged package complete with scheduled tours. Every detail of each day of the trip will be carefully spelled out on the itinerary. Forget about renting bikes and backpacking around the countryside. Improvised activities are too unpredictable for the "control-freak" Hazard Five individual.

Along with the limitations, there are several advantages to the Hazard Five's logical style. For one, people come to rely on your dependability. If you say you will be somewhere at 4:00 P.M., you will be there, perhaps earlier, but not later than 4:00 P.M. You are also a compulsively organized individual who keeps things in their rightful place. If a bank mistakenly sends you a late-charge notice for an auto payment, you will quickly produce the check (which, of course, *was* on time), and send a detailed letter to the bank explaining the nature of their error. You will no doubt accompany this note with a phone call, duly noting the name of the individual you spoke to, being sure to address your letter to this individual's attention. Such qualities also make you great workers. Always on time, fastidious about completing assignments according to an established standard, employers can count on your predictable job performance.

But even being organized, reliable, and prompt can have its downside. Consider the case of Warren, a 26-year-old man who sought out my services because Sharon, his wife of two years, was fed up with her husband's "controlling ways." Although she saw Warren as a solid provider and a man she knew she could always count on, there were aspects of his personality that she could no longer tolerate. For instance, Sharon liked vacations that consisted of historic sightseeing; Warren was content to lie by the ocean and read novels. Sharon wanted to spend some money to fix up their apartment; Warren wanted to save every possible penny to put toward the purchase of a house of their own. Sharon liked to let housecleaning chores pile up during the busy workweek and get the place tidied up on the weekend; Warren preferred to stay on top of the housecleaning, and insisted that the beds be made and the carpets vacuumed each and every day.

The differences this couple faced might have been workable had Warren been willing to compromise. But he was not. And his unwillingness was not just about a stubborn insistence on having things his way. From Warren's perspective, he *had* to do things his way. Without the predictability and structure that he was afforded by his rituals, Warren felt he had no control over his life. He did not realize it, but his need for routine was his method for distracting himself from more primary control needs.

When a Hazard Five individual's routine is altered, he experiences anxiety. Anxiety is a normal emotion that everyone experiences, and there are healthy and unhealthy ways of attempting to control it. As a Hazard Five individual, Warren felt that if his rituals were in order, his life was in order. As a Hazard Five golfer, Lee believed that if he studied and mastered every aspect of his golf swing, he would be able to control the outcome of his shots. Both Warren and Lee were wrong.

In this life, we are more powerless than we usually care to admit. We can work hard and lay the groundwork for the kind of life we would like to have, but the outcome for our effort is not always within our control. Beyond a certain point, for instance, you cannot control your children, your health, or even the flight of a golf ball. This is not to say that working hard to realize goals is not a reasonable and healthy pursuit. But remember that even though it might be true that God helps those that help themselves, there are no guarantees. Be the best parent you can be and work hard at your golf game. Just don't be shocked if your kids turn out differently than you had planned. And don't be surprised if after a substantial investment in the study of the fundamentals, and hours of hard work at the practice tee, you find yourself frozen over a golf ball, your body unable to release and attack, your mind and spirit unwilling to take the risk that is a part of surrendering control.

Use Both Sides of Your Brain

DURING THE PAST TWENTY YEARS, THERE HAS BEEN A GREAT DEAL of research on the differences between the functions of the left and right hemispheres of the brain. It has been determined that the left side of the brain regulates logical, sequential, and analytical thinking while the right hemisphere is responsible for processing emotions and creativity. Almost all individuals are dominant in either left *or* right brain functioning. Individuals who are left-side dominant often end up in professions such as computer programming, engineering, dentistry, or accounting. Individuals who are right brain dominant are more likely to become involved in music, dance, or creative writing. Beyond vocational pursuit, whether you are right as opposed to left brain dominant has a significant impact on the manner in which you approach your golf game as well as your life in general.

The game of golf—if it is to be played well—requires the use of both sides of the brain. The thought patterns of Hazard Five golfers are mostly dominated by the logic of the brain's left hemisphere. Lee represents a perfect example. He was a master of the checklist of quantified details that are handled by the left side of the brain and was more than ready to step into his shot. Unfortunately, when he had to "shift hemispheres" and let the golf swing happen, he could not pull the trigger. He became afraid to let go and simply *feel* his golf swing.

"Right brain" golfers play the game by feel. They are more adept at sensing the *whole* swing rather than breaking it down into fragments. Unlike the overanalytical Hazard Five golfer, these more "free-spirited," spontaneous types of individuals just step up to their ball and let it rip. When taken to an extreme, this approach can also create problems. Ever see a golfer strike the ball beautifully, thirty yards wide of the target, only to exclaim afterward, "I was aimed that way. Got to check my alignment." Similar problems can occur with regard to club selection and the gauging of conditions such as wind, pin placement, and course conditions. Right brain golfers tend to skip over the checklist that is necessary during the preshot phase of their game.

The first extensive discussion of the need to apply the "whole brain" for playing effective golf was presented by Gary Wiren and Richard Coop in their 1978 book entitled *The New Golf Mind.* They referred to the left hemisphere as the "analyzer," and the right hemisphere as the "integrator." The analyzer was responsible for analysis of playing conditions, preshot routine, club selection, hole strategy, and alignment. The integrator handled the visualization of ball flight, flight distance, feel, touch, tempo, and imagination on trouble shots. It was their contention that "A lot of golfers play the game almost exclusively with one hemisphere or the other, which is the mental equivalent of playing with a half set of clubs."

Professional golfers are also dominated by a left versus right brain approach to their games. Tom Kite and Nick Faldo are renowned as master students of their golf swings. Always looking to fine-tune their mechanics, these hardworking golfers spend countless hours at the practice range. Ben Hogan is noted as one of golf history's great analyzers of the golf swing. His classic book, *The Modern Fundamentals of Golf,* is often referred to as the consummate statement about the mechanical side of golf.

On the other side are golfers such as Sam Snead, Ben Crenshaw, and Seve Ballesteros. These golfers *feel* the golf swing and are more content to play than to practice. If they make a mistake on the golf course, it's more likely to be the result of improper setup or a misread of course conditions. When Sam Snead was once asked how he hit a draw, he responded "I think draw." It's highly unlikely that Mr. Snead ever found the need to read Mr. Hogan's classic best-seller.

The advantage the pros have over recreational golfers is that they know their games and they know themselves. A Hazard Five professional like Tom Kite fully understands that his emphasis on fundamentals can be a problem at times, and he can balance his game when he needs to. When the game of a feel player like Ben Crenshaw begins to come apart, he knows that he had better give more time and attention to his setup checklist. Bill Moretti, who is Director of the Academy of Golf Dynamics in Austin, Texas, recommends that when the weekend golfer's game starts to suffer, "Your best bet is to take a lesson from the other guy: Mr. Analytical, think intuitively, Mr. Intuitive, check your mechanics."

There is nothing wrong with the responsible behavior that is a by-product of being a highly organized, list-keeping, left-brained individual. However, like all psychological qualities that have been discussed in this book, the determination of healthy as opposed to not healthy often comes down to a matter of degree. If your need for order is compulsive—that is, you are *compelled* to follow routines and require that others comply with your needs—the matter has gotten out of hand. In order to strike the balance necessary for healthy interpersonal relationships as well as for a complete golf game, you need to explore the intuitive, creative, right brain side of life. You need to surrender some of the science of logic and delve more into the art of letting go.

The Art of Letting Go

As a Hazard Five golfer, how do you begin the process of learning to be more spontaneous, to further trust your instincts, to let go? I learned something on the subject after a seminar that I had presented to a group of assistant golf professionals. I had been talking about playing in "The Zone," and had concluded with the comment, "Work hard at your game, stay with your routine, and let go of the results. It's out of your hands."

Afterward, a member of the audience approached me and noted, "Your orientation sounds a lot like the Twelve Steps. I'm a recovering alcoholic and have attended AA for two years now. I've never really integrated golf with addictions and recovery before."

"That's interesting," I responded. "Neither have I."

Until that moment.

For years, I had referred my patients to Twelve Step programs to help them recover from various addictions. The programs are based on the notion that addicts are powerless over not just their addiction, but many things in life. The spiritually based orientation encourages its participants to "turn over to a Higher Power" the things in their lives which they have no control over. Twelve Step programs make use of slogans such as *Let go and let God, One day at a time, Progress not perfection, Easy does it,* and *Keep it simple.* The more I considered it, the more I realized that these principles were readily applicable to the game of golf.

Hazard Five golfers believe that through hard work and persistence, they can control their games. Ever hear the alcoholic in denial state that "I could stop drinking anytime I want to?" Not that alcoholism and Hazard Five golf tendencies are entirely comparable, but there is a common controlling component that does apply to both addictive behavior and the need to be in control on the golf course. Along these lines, if you recognize yourself as a Hazard Five golfer, the first step in your personal recovery from the need to be in control just might be the same as the first of the Twelve Steps for recovering addicts. That is, the admission that you too are powerless, not necessarily over a substance such as alcohol or cocaine, but more likely over the need to be in control. Add to this admission the recognition that you are also powerless over your ability to control the flight of a golf ball with the consistent accuracy and authority you so desperately desire.

Individuals who stay with Twelve Step programs talk about a fascinating development that occurs during the course of their recovery. By relinquishing or letting go of the effort to control the people, places, and things that define their lives, they actually were rewarded by gaining more control. Remember those hollow, cylinder-shaped "Chinese handcuffs" that we played with as kids? You placed each of your index fingers in opposite ends of the multicolored tube. When you attempted to pull your fingers out, they became more stuck. The harder you pulled, the tighter the "handcuffs" gripped around your fingers. Only by relaxing and then gently pulling apart, did your fingers release. By not trying so hard, you were rewarded with the control and freedom necessary to pull your fingers free.

To understand the art of letting go, it is necessary to understand the paradox of control and surrender. How many times, after a horrible tee shot, have you teed up another, quickly swiped at it, and hit a good shot? This experience perfectly illustrates the phenomenon of gaining control by relinquishing it. Because you were disgusted with the first shot, and didn't even care about the second, you stopped trying so hard. When you got to this point of "giving up," you were actually practicing the art of "letting go" and allowing your inner self to do its thing, uncluttered by the usual presence of your strong willful self.

Viktor Frankl, a Nazi death camp survivor, was a psychotherapist who developed a psychological technique that he referred to as paradoxical intention. The technique consisted of advising his patients to do the very thing they feared and to do so to an extreme degree. In Frankl's book, *Man's Search for Meaning*, he described the case of a young doctor that he was treating because of a fear of sweating in public places. Frankl . . . "advised the patient, in the event that sweating should recur, to resolve deliberately to show people how much he could sweat." His approach was based on both helping the patient appreciate the humor of the predicament and illustrating the inherent paradox of the situation. It is interesting that Frankl developed these ideas while in the powerless state of being a prisoner in a concentration camp. The lesson he learned and applied to the technique of paradoxical intention was that although you might not always be able to control your fate, you can at the very least take some kind of stand. Even if this stand requires that you surrender to a situation that you want absolutely no part of.

I had the opportunity to test the technique of paradoxical intention on a golfer with a 3 handicap who came to me for help with the mental side of his game the week before his club championship. Dennis was concerned because he had been pushing all his woods and long irons off to the right for the past two weeks. He recognized that he was getting himself all worked up about the upcoming championship and that his problems were quickly extending into the psychological realm. He scheduled an appointment to see me, requesting that I teach him a self-hypnotic technique. I complied with this request, but also suggested that he stay off the practice range until the morning of his first match. I recognized Dennis's Hazard Five qualities of overanalysis and excessive practice habits, and wanted to settle down his left brain intensity. One final suggestion I made was that on the day of his match, he make every effort to push the ball as far to the right as he possibly could. Needless to say, we debated this point for quite a while before Dennis understood the motivation behind my unusual request and finally agreed to go along with the plan. It was obvious that despite his skeptical compliance with my suggestion, he was, on some level, relieved with my directive to intentionally push his golf shots. Dennis had no problem believing that he *could* manage to push the ball right. As a Hazard Five golfer, Dennis actually felt some degree of relief. He once again felt in control of the situation.

Dennis did not win his club championship. In fact, he didn't even make it to the final match. But Dennis was happy because he knew he had played well. And he did learn something that made the entire experience worthwhile. Trying hard to push the ball right, he hit most every fairway down the middle. Dennis learned a valuable lesson about control, surrender, and paradox. He learned that within him lies an oppositional force that stubbornly opposes his willful desires. And that sometimes, a little bit of old-fashioned reverse psychology is the only way to successfully outwit this power within.

You might not always feel comfortable about the use of paradoxical intention on the golf course, but if you are going to make progress with the art of letting go, you at the very least have to develop an attitude of acceptance when you go out to play. You must come to appreciate the reality that the best you can do is work hard, give it your best shot, and then accept the outcome. At first you will fight this attitude, but eventually you will find that there is a peace and serenity that comes from this resignation. Another slogan that is associated with Twelve Step programs is, *"I didn't quit, I surrendered."* Think about it. There *is* a difference.

Common among professional athletes after a significant victory is an expression of appreciation toward God. These gifted athletes appreciate that their talents are God-given and also recognize the host of fateful circumstances that must be in place in order to secure victory away from other very talented athletes. Sam Snead never won the U.S. Open, but did manage four second-place finishes. It has been determined that if he shot 69 at each of the final rounds of his appearances, he would have won nine U.S. Open titles. In response to this fact, Snead was quoted as saying, "I believe in destiny . . . what's going to be is going to be. If I'm going to win, I'm going to win . . . I don't give a damn what the other guy shoots. I'm going to win if it's my turn."

And then there's the story of Sylvester "Cy" Young, the one-armed golfer who accomplished two holes-in-one during one round of golf. When asked how he accomplished such an incredibly improbable feat, his response was "Pure luck." Call it luck if you will, but I am inclined to believe that the lessons learned by Mr. Young in the sometimes joyous, sometimes cruel games of golf *and* of life included an understanding of the things that he could and *could not* control. Albeit with only one arm, Mr. Sylvester "Cy" Young apparently understands what it means to "let go" and give it his best shot. Only then can you see what the gods have planned for the particular occasion.

Find a Trigger

LEARNING TO "LET GO" AND LET YOUR GOLF SWING HAPPEN DOES not occur overnight. For Hazard Five golfers, whose left brain dominance has been mechanically "in control" for many years, learning to trust yourself, to have faith in the outcome of your shot, will likely take a while to accomplish. In the meanwhile, there are a couple of shortcuts that can be helpful while you are in the process of developing a more intuitive feel for the game.

Nothing is of greater help to the Hazard Five golfer—whose tendency is to freeze over the ball—than the use of a trigger. A trigger is a physical action or thought that signals the beginning of the golf swing. Most important, a trigger enables the shift from left brain analysis to right brain action. In effect, the trigger helps you cross the boundary that separates voluntary control from the "no-brain" self-trust necessary to put a good stroke on the ball.

There are a wide range of possible forms that the trigger can take. John Daly quickly became identified by his aggressive verbal triggers of "grip it and rip it" or "kill it." It doesn't matter what you actually say to yourself at this critical moment, just before you begin the golf swing. Try "let it loose, Mother Goose," "away we go," or simply count to three if it suits you. Most important is that you *always* get that club moving in response to the verbal trigger you have designated for yourself.

Another popular trigger is a physical cue such as the forward press. This refers to making a physical move *toward* the target, before beginning the process of pulling the club *away* from this point of destination. Some golfers shift their hips, others angle their wrists. The theory behind the forward press was well described by Harvey Penick, who found the technique to be useful physically as well as psychologically. Mr. Penick compared the golf swing with the swinging of a bucket. He said that "If you're going to swing this bucket back like a golf backswing, you just naturally won't do it from a dead stop. Your hands and hips and shoulders and legs will rock forward a tiny bit to provide the reaction that gives momentum to the backswing."

Whether you use a forward press or not, find some signal that will make you pull the trigger and then stick with it. If Lee, our Hazard Five case-study golfer, had committed to a trigger, he could not have possibly stood frozen over his ball for so long. Even if he gently tightened his grip or said to himself "here goes nothing," and then made good on his commitment to begin the swing, his game would have improved immeasurably. He might have made some bad shots, but wasn't this the case anyway?

Recognize that as a Hazard Five golfer, you will fight this technique. The employment of a trigger is designed to help you surrender control, and this will at first make you feel uncomfortable. Do not abandon the approach if it fails to help you right away. Remember that what you are attempting to accomplish is the ability to "let it go" during a critical moment of truth which is so vital to the eventual success of your plans for improving your game.

Develop a Preshot Routine

THE TRIGGER CAN BE THE FINAL STEP OF A MORE ELABORATE PRE-shot routine. As a Hazard Five golfer, the preshot routine should come relatively easy to you, in that this highly structured sequence of behaviors and thoughts fits right in with left brain functioning. Although virtually every professional golfer has a detailed preshot routine, very few recreational golfers have incorporated this very important process into their golf games.

The preshot routine, so long as it is capped off with a trigger, will help feed the Hazard Five golfer's need for order and control. In fact, such a routine will help alleviate many of the problems associated with most of Golf's Mental Hazards because it is a predictable sequence of behaviors that is invariably repeated before each and every stroke. The golfer's night-light, if you will. Whether you feel fear, anger, self-consciousness, or despair, you can always count on the deeply programmed preshot routine to be there for you.

Of course, in order for it to become deeply programmed and hence automatic, it will have to be vigilantly employed. This means that before every shot, even on the practice range, you must go through the exact same routine. It has been said that Jack Nicklaus's routine is so precise that if you followed him around the golf course with a stopwatch, the time it took him to pull a club out of his bag and actually hit the ball would never vary by more than a second. There are many variations on the preshot routine. The following is one example:

1. When you arrive at the ball, place your bag or cart in the same place (in relation to the ball) every time. This will set the rest of your routine in motion.
2. Study the shot. Examine the lie, determine the yardage, estimate the force of the wind.
3. Choose a club to hit. Make sure you are not indecisive. Remove it from the bag and stand behind your ball, looking down the target line.

4. Visualize the shot you want to hit and take a full cleansing breath.
5. Slowly approach the ball and step in with your right foot first, then with your left. Make sure you are properly aligned.
6. Look up at the target and then down at your ball two times. Enact your trigger and begin the swing.

This suggested routine is one of literally thousands you can develop for your own personal style. The critical factor common to all effective preshot routines is that they be consistently repeatable. A point worth additional emphasis deals with the destructive potential of indecision. If you are between clubs, briefly think it through, pick one, and don't look back. If you decide to "cut the legs off" rather than pitch-and-run a thirty-yarder, stick with this decision. Even the pros get in trouble when they go back to their bags to grab another club. It might be the wrong club, or your decision to go over a tree instead of coming around it left-to-right might not work, but at least your mind will not be distracted by the drain of indecision.

The Worst That Can Happen

THE MOST DEBILITATING CONCERN FOR THE GOLFER WHO NEEDS TO be in control is the horrifying outcome—the ugly shot. Unfortunately, our greatest fears are often prophetic. It is for this reason that Hazard Five golfers do well by taking a "what's the worst that can happen" attitude toward every shot. This ties in with the paradoxical thinking that was discussed in an earlier portion of this chapter. If you acknowledge that hitting a horrible golf shot will not signal the end of the world, your life, or even your golf round, the oppositional demon that resides in your subconscious just might let you slide on by and escape the "catastrophic" outcome. Consider the well-quoted words of Cary Middlecoff on the subject: "I always think before an important shot: What is the worst thing that can happen on this shot? I can whiff it, shank it, or hit it out-of-bounds. But even if one of these bad things happens, I've got a little money in the bank, my wife still loves me, and my dog won't bite me when I come home."

8

HAZARD SIX:
An Unwillingness to Work

"Minds, like bodies, will often fall into a
pimpled, ill-conditioned state from mere
excess of comfort."

—CHARLES DICKENS

Freddy loves the big ball. To him, there's nothing better than smacking it on the screws with his driver, watching it rise, suspend, shift into overdrive, and then pause briefly before beginning its descent. He doesn't hit 'em that way all the time, but when he does, it's a thing of beauty. And he loves the reactions of others. The oohs and aahs; "Freddy can really hit a golf ball, can't he?" Since he was a teen, his driving prowess had always gotten people excited.

*At age 36, the legs unwilling to cooperate on the softball fields of the bar leagues, Fred has finally decided to get serious about his golf game. That's where it's at for him and his pushing forty peers. And besides, Fred hardly has a senior game. He can still smack that driver to the tune of 260, maybe 270 yards. But now, for the first time in his life, he is going to get serious about the **whole** game and become a complete golfer.*

The pro, Alex, tells Fred that because of his good eye-hand coordination, he usually makes solid contact and because of his wrist action and weight shift, when he does catch one, it will go a long way. But his fundamentals are all messed up. If he doesn't put some time in and regroove some bad habits, he'll never hit the ball with any kind of consistency. And if he wants to score, he needs to work on his short game: chipping and putting.

Alex gives Freddy a drill. While at the range, hit twenty-five 8-irons with half swings, pretending the ball is a clockface, hitting it at "one'o'clock" to make sure he doesn't come over the top, across the ball. That's the reason for Fred's big slice, Alex tells him.

Freddy decides to practice more and play less. He'll play with his regular foursome on Sundays, but will remain true to his new swing. Alex had told him that motor memory was a hard thing to change at his age. The habits he picked up as a kid, whacking balls with his friends, were deeply ingrained, so when he was tired or struggling, he would likely fall back on these old ways. The only remedy was to hit thousands upon thousands of balls, until his body could remember nothing except that smooth new inside-out swing.

Wednesday evening at the range, Fred finds a spot on level ground. He loosens up quickly, takes out his 8-iron, and hits a few nice and easy shots, straight up and out, about 135 yards of carry. Then he hits one fat, sending a jolt into his wrists, up his arms. He comes over the top on the next one, taking too full a swing. Fred remembers to think "one'o'clock," but still takes a full swing and the ball slices. This is crazy, thinks Fred. What the heck is wrong? Still determined, he tries his 5-iron a few times, but it's useless. He's all out of sync.

Fred takes a break on the bench and watches the early summer sun descend, casting long, distorted shadows of the few golfers who remain at the range. He studies them. Each is so serious about the game, each thinks his game is so damn important. Fred has to laugh as he watches one older fellow. Every shot is a major production. Stretching, tightening the Velcro on his glove, standing behind the ball, going through this painstaking routine, before hitting maybe one shot every five minutes. And it was a weak shot at that.

Fred begins to feel hungry. It's been a long day. He pulls his driver out of his bag and tees one up. Yeah, golf is supposed to be fun, he thinks. What the heck am I trying to prove? He walks up to his ball, and without waiting, takes a giant rip at it. He catches it all. One of his patented drives that his friends would kill to be able to hit. Fred holds his finish and watches the ball, still in flight. He imagines the cutters and slashers behind him, in awe of his power. I've got a game, thinks Fred. I've got a damn good game.

Are you a dreamer like Fred? Do you have goals, secret successes that you harbor, that you just never seem to find the time to get around to? Maybe you don't believe you're talented enough, or maybe, as Fred did, you have managed to convince yourself that you really don't care about the particular goal. Maybe you're right. Not everyone has the same need for achievement, and in fact, many individuals are content with the life they have, unencumbered by the mental demands of striving to be more than they already are.

If your score for the Hazard Six portion of the *MHAS* was in the elevated range, you probably *do* strive to overcome the lack of focus and ambition that are necessary for game improvement. You could go the route that Fred did, and play the old "sour-grapes" number. But let's face it, Fred *did* care and so do you. You never would have come this far along in this book if you did not wish to find a way to stick to your goals, improve your game, and finally conquer the enemy that is yourself.

Hazard Six Characteristics

EVER SINCE I WAS A KID, I HAVE WANTED TO WRITE A BOOK. WHEN I was 8 years old, I sent a copy of my manuscript, *Medicine Marches On*, complete with stick-figure illustrations, to Random House. A good-natured secretary accurately identified the situation and responded with a kind and supportive note (to the extent to which a rejection to even 8-year-old boys can be kind and supportive), which concluded with the statement, "I'm sure you will write a wonderful book someday."

Thirty-three years later I began to write. Looking back, I realize that the reason it took me so long to begin was that I lacked the maturity and patience to deal with the frustration, hard work, criticism, and rejection that were a necessary part of the writing process. In my 20s, I lay on the sofa and conjured up titles for scores of books, all brilliant, of course, but unfortunately I was too caught up watching *Andy Griffith* reruns to follow through and generate any text to go along with the titles.

In my 30s, I became more serious. I would have an idea, buy a new pen (preferably an expensive one) and notebook and after procrastinating for a week or two, finally sit down and render a handful of first paragraphs. But something was wrong. It didn't come easily or naturally for me. So I figured that it was not meant to be or that I was just not that talented a writer, and I would abandon the project.

Finally, at the age of 41, I became a writer. Which is to say that I spent time writing. It took three years of steady effort and literally hundreds of rejections before I stumbled upon the concept for this book and managed to sell the idea. Here I sit today, as I do everyday, sometimes feeling the joy of fluid, creative thoughts, other times cursing at the computer monitor in frustration. But the one thing that does not change is the fact that I put my time in, each day, every day.

Writing and golf both have their ups and downs. What the two activities also have in common is that making progress requires hard, painstaking work. Good, steady golf requires concentration and a lot of bear-down intensity and effort. And game improvement—particularly for those like Fred who have developed some bad habits—requires a committed work ethic. Hazard Six golfers, who put little time or effort into the accomplishment of goals, who are not driven toward success, who practice the parts of their game that least require practice, do not understand the "no pain, no gain" nature of growth.

Hazard Six golfers like Fred desire improvement. But they want it to come easily. Like the adolescent who wants to be a famous rock star after only a couple of guitar lessons, they do not comprehend the hard work that any kind of success requires. Always desiring life to be hassle-free and smooth, the Hazard Six individual cannot tolerate discomfort and does not know what it means to suffer. By always avoiding problems and trying to make life *easier*, they actually suffer *more* than if they were to simply face life's problems head on.

The famous first paragraph in M. Scott Peck's classic bestseller, *The Road Less Traveled*, simply states, "Life is difficult." The author goes on to describe life as a series of problems that require discipline in order to be successfully solved. One of the tools necessary to accomplish this discipline involves learning to delay gratification. Dr. Peck describes this as "a process of scheduling the pain and pleasure of life in such a way as to enhance the pleasure by meeting and experiencing the pain first and getting it over with."

The child who saves the frosting on the cake for last, or the busy executive who makes a difficult and dreaded phone call before engaging in the more pleasant activity of processing favorable profit and loss numbers are examples of the principle of delaying gratification. I, for example, never play *Microsoft Golf for Windows* until I have completed my daily quota of writing. No small task when you consider I just added Pebble Beach and Mauna Kea to my collection of courses!

As a Hazard Six individual, you are lacking in the ability to delay gratification. You might delay a host of odd jobs that have to be completed around the house in favor of reading the paper, watching a ball game, or running out to the mall to spend a few bucks on some unnecessary purchase. While behavior such as watching television before getting around to the completion of homework might reflect "normal" adolescent behavior, your own "adult" behavior should be beyond this stage.

As golfers, you will practice areas of your game that you are most adept at. Tasks that are the least bit tedious will be seen as boring or unnecessary. Hazard Six golfers like Fred cannot take a step back to change an old, undesirable habit and delay the gratification of instant success. They want to feel *good*, and they want to feel good *now!* Of course, the quest for immediate gratification fails miserably in the end. Fred felt good when he boomed a big drive. But how long did the good feeling last before he was once again cursing those golfers who, with less raw talent, continued to take his money?

It can be argued that Hazard Six types are simply lazy, unmotivated, not driven toward success. I disagree. I believe that there is no such thing as laziness. Beneath what appears as lazy, unmotivated behavior are issues of fear. Whereas the Hazard One golfer fears the feeling of fear, and the Hazard Four golfer fears social embarrassment, the Hazard Six golfer fears putting in the time and effort only to be dissatisfied and disappointed with the end result. Those of you who are Hazard Six golfers might claim that you are unwilling to invest in the improvement of your game because you don't care or because you don't have the time. But beyond these explanations are apprehensions. Deep-rooted, well-concealed, fearful apprehensions about not measuring up, about failing, and yes, even about succeeding. At the heart of an unwillingness to work, of procrastination or an apparent lack of motivation, is the real fear that you might give it your best shot only to discover that the very best you can accomplish is mediocrity.

Fear of Failure

STAN IS A 25-YEAR-OLD MAN WHO SOUGHT OUT MY SERVICES TO help him better understand the problems he was having at work. A stockbroker and investment counselor, Stan was in danger of being discharged from his company. He was not managing to cultivate new accounts and was even starting to lose some long-term clients who had expressed dissatisfaction with the quality of service he was providing.

Talking to Stan during our first meeting, I could see that he had all the tools for success in the investment business. He had a good appearance, was very articulate, warm, and personable. And he appeared to know what he was talking about. I discovered that Stan had graduated from a top-notch school with a degree in business and in the top 10 percent of his class. He toyed with the idea of going to law school, but his love for the stock market and his drive for the unpredictability and excitement of the investment world led him instead to an MBA. He successfully completed the program in two years time, again near the top of his class.

During his first year of work, Stan succeeded in arranging more interviews than the other three new brokers combined. This is the point where Stan's problems began. After aggressively pursuing a lead, he would often be late for a meeting or cancel it at the last minute. During recent weeks, he had gone so far as to not even show up for a few appointments. In addition to these problems, he was skipping seminars and found himself unable to get around to reading company literature. Stan had never before been a procrastinator. He was perplexed and scared by his recent pattern of behavior.

Rather than take you through all the psychotherapy involved, let it suffice to say that Stan had a rather severe fear of failure. Going through school and getting his foot in the door of a major investment company were intermediary steps along the route to success. But he was now facing a bottom-line moment. No longer studying theoretical cases presented in textbooks and class-rooms, he was responsible for real people and their money. And they were depending on his expertise to guide them. School and job interviews were child's play compared with this do-or-die point in Stan's life.

Stan's uncharacteristically irresponsible approach to his work provided him with a form of comfort. It enabled him to believe that his ability was better than what was being reflected in his performance. If the numbers did not look good, he could always blame it on the fact that he was disorganized or unmotivated, that he was not giving his best effort. It was more desirable for Stan to see himself as lazy than as a failure, for in Stan's mind, failure was a permanent stamp that could not be explained away.

Let's go back to Fred and his lackadaisical approach to golf improvement. See any similarities? While the stakes for Fred might not be as severe as the stakes for Stan, both were using their unwillingness to work as a way to avoid the dreaded fear of failing. Stan experienced anxiety and guilt in response to his inability to accomplish his goals, while Fred pretended he did not care. These might seem like rather extreme self-destructive ways to skirt the failure issue, but remember what is at stake in the minds of these two men. If either Fred or Stan worked hard at his goals and came up short of what he expected of himself or what he perceived as others' expectations for him, it would have sent him the distorted message that he was a totally worthless human being.

Hazard Six individuals typically think very little of them-selves. They procrastinate to avoid the unpleasantness of these negative feelings, but only succeed in eliminating any chances for success. If you scored high on this scale, count your blessings if your shoddy work habits do not extend beyond your golf game. But the chances are they do. Maybe you *should* put more time into your short game, but take a moment to examine other areas of your life that you would love to see change for the better but that you tell yourself are not that important, that you just don't have enough time to pursue, or that simply cannot be changed.

Before you commit to changing anything in your life, you must first realize that it will not come without a substantial

effort. Chances are, if you ever dream about having a more intimate relationship, a more responsible job, or a lower handicap,
you *really do* want it. Of course, it is easier to pretend you don't
care or to convince yourself that it's just not meant to be.
Whether you do something about it or not, don't lie to yourself.
The truth might not be pleasant, but the discomfort you experience could serve as the motivation to examine and eventually
overcome your fear of failing. As a golfing friend of mine likes
to say about life and risk-taking: "This ain't no dress rehearsal!"
And he's right. When you're old, reflecting back on your life, it
is unlikely that you'll regret risks you took that did not pan out.
If you are afraid to fail, recognize that failing has nothing to do
with outcome. The only way you can fail is if you never take the
risk.

The Problem of Perfectionism

ONE OF MY BEST AND OLDEST FRIENDS FRUSTRATES THE HECK OUT
of me because he refuses to take his golf game more seriously.
He plays maybe three or four times a season, and when he does
go out, he is content with a handful of decent moments, and
claims that he is satisfied with the role that golf plays in his life.
His attitude might sound healthy and balanced, but I just cannot
buy it. I've known him for twenty-five years and I refuse to
accept his laid-back attitude about golf

I always score better than this friend, and I know he believes
that if he put any time into the game at all, he would be a better
golfer than I am. He doesn't come right out and say it—in fact,
we haven't even gotten around to discussing this entire matter
—but I know how he feels about it all. I know because I was
there to observe the pride he tried so hard to disguise the day
when he was the only member of our foursome to par the first-
handicap hole. I know because I've seen his constrained joy
when he picks up his tee after a big drive. I know because of the
way his chest swells with pride after knocking an approach onto
the green from 175 yards out.

But, of course, these moments are few and far between because
my friend doesn't really like golf that much. More often than
not, he hits shanks and hooks, and struggles through periods of

ineptness that can last for several holes or even an entire round. On these days, my "laid-back" buddy bears the look of an embattled warrior who has just returned from defeat. But, of course, it doesn't "really matter," because he is content to play a few times a year, to maybe hit a few good shots, and have a few laughs.

I know that it's none of my business whether my friend is in denial. I do leave him alone on the subject (except for a sweatshirt I bought him for his forty-fourth birthday that says, *Denial: It's not a river in Egypt,* which by the way, I've never seen him wear). But this is my book and I can say anything I want on these pages. I know that my friend has perfectionist qualities or a very low tolerance for mediocrity. He wants to excel at everything he does, and he believes that this level of excellence should come with relative ease. Would he like to beat me when we go out to play? You bet he would! But considering that golf is a game that is based more on misses than on successful moments, I don't think he could manage to live through the process of getting to that point. And so it is the case with all perfectionists. They often appear as disinterested, lazy types who do not really care about success when the truth is that if they cannot be perfect, they would rather withdraw from the process entirely. Anything is better than the dreaded affliction of being simply mediocre.

If you are the prototypic Hazard Six individual, it is very likely that you are a perfectionist. You might find this hard to believe in light of the fact that you probably tend to procrastinate and generally view yourself as being lazy. Bear in mind, however, that perfectionism has less to do with your behavior than with your attitude. In fact, successful, hardworking people are typically less perfectionist and have more realistic goals than the average individual. You want impeccable results and you expect them to occur very quickly. But the reality is that very few things in this world come easily, and if you cannot tolerate batting less than 1.000, you probably will drift toward the tendency to not bat at all.

The Unconscious Fear of Success

THE FEAR OF FAILURE AND PERFECTIONISM ARE CONCEPTS WHICH are easy to comprehend as they pertain to an unwillingness to work. A bit more complicated and difficult to fathom is why anyone in his right mind would be afraid to succeed. Yet this is a very common unconscious reaction that forms the basis for what might appear as unmotivated or lazy behavior.

Tony was an assistant golf professional who was regarded as being one of the better players in his region. He came to see me because of a disturbing awareness that he tended to play badly when he was in the lead. To Tony, it almost seemed as if he did not want to win. An example came during his last tournament when Tony shot a 68 to lead the first round and opened with a pair of birdies on the second day.

On the tee of the par-three 16th, still two strokes ahead, Tony again got that uneasy feeling and pulled his tee shot well left of the green into deep rough. He ended up tripling the 16th, and despite parring the last two holes, eventually finished second in the tournament, one stroke behind the winner. What bothered Tony more than the errant tee shot, or even the loss of the tournament, was the fact that choking when in the lead was becoming a pattern. To his way of thinking, it was almost as if he was *afraid* of winning.

The result of counseling yielded the fact that Tony did in fact fear success. He was 29 years old, had been happily married for five years with a 2-year-old son, and his wife and he were planning on a second child in the near future. Tony enjoyed working at the club that employed him and looked forward to a position as a head professional at some point in the future. His wife made a decent salary working as a nurse, so money was not a big problem. He felt established in his community and had plenty of family in the vicinity. So why the fear?

Tony was a gifted golfer. He probably worked less on his game than most of the other golfers that he usually outplayed. Other professionals in the region touted Tony as one of the few area pros who stood a chance to someday reach the Tour. But Tony liked his life the way it was. He was afraid of the changes that would result if he was too successful. He would have to leave his wife and son in order to travel and he would also need to devote much more time to practice. Tony enjoyed playing with his son, going to the movies with his wife on Saturday nights, and having Sunday dinner at his in-laws. He was afraid that success would force him into a life of a workaholic, complete with extensive traveling, living in hotels, and eating in restaurants.

There is a tendency to assume that, so far as achievement is concerned, more is better. But this is not always the case. Tony's wife attended my final session with him, during which time he expressed his honest feelings to her. He was amazed that she did not find him to be unambitious or lazy because of his lack of drive, and she was shocked to hear that he did not really wish to be a Tour player.

The lesson to be learned from the case of Tony is that there are no "etched in stone" standards for success. Tony elected to leave his life as it was. The reason his decision was the correct one was that it was based on self-honesty. But before you tell yourself that your unwillingness to work at your career, relationships, or your golf game is based on a desire to not become too intensely caught up in these matters, think again. Consider that success is not black or white. If you are a 20-handicapper who does not have the time to work your way down to scoring in the 70s, you might have a legitimate case. Be honest with yourself, but don't write off all goals because the most ambitious is not realistically obtainable.

Are You Deserving of Success?

ASIDE FROM LACK OF DESIRE OR FEAR OF BECOMING A WORKAholic, there are other unconscious motives for fearing success. Consider, for instance, that it's lonely at the top. Successful individuals have to adjust to the reality that friends, associates, even family will be resentful and jealous of their success. Have you ever withheld information about a salary increase from a friend whom you already make more money than, or failed to mention to a good friend who hasn't dated in months that you just met someone wonderful? And why do golfers typically play up or down to the level of their playing partners?

The answer could be that you unconsciously avoid success based on guilt or a feeling that you are undeserving of any kind of success. There are many people who sabotage their success through procrastination and disorganization because in their unconscious mind they feel uncomfortable and undeserving of the good feelings that accompany success. An extreme example is reflected in the case of David, whose son died in an automobile accident at the age of 3. Even though David was in no way responsible for the actions of the drunken driver in the other car, he still felt enormous guilt for not managing in some way to save his son's life. He also felt guilty about having survived the crash himself.

Seven years after the fatal accident, David still does not permit himself to experience enjoyment. He was in the running for a sales-related bonus trip to Hawaii that his company was offering. Six weeks before the numbers were to be totaled, David's sales dropped suddenly. If you asked him about it, he would tell you that he did not do it intentionally. But the truth is that he unconsciously did not believe himself worthy of an all-expenses-paid vacation.

Even if you did not experience a tragedy as devastating as David's, you can still fall prey to an unconscious fear of success based on guilt. Do you tend to sabotage pleasurable feelings? When things are going well, do you muster up a negative slant on matters or wait for the other shoe to drop? This is not an uncommon reaction, and its roots go into the details of your past, well beyond the scope of this book. But if you do relate to the experience of excessive guilt, consider that you might be repressing an unconscious fear of being successful. A fear that might on the surface give the behavioral appearance of procrastination, laziness, or a generally poor work ethic.

The experience of guilt is more often than not well out of proportion with the circumstances that you feel guilty about. Think about what it is that you have done in your past or present life that you feel guilty about and consider the possibility that these feelings might be unsubstantiated. Of course, some degree of guilt is healthy as well as necessary for the maintenance of social order. But you *are* probably worthy of the good feelings that accompany hard work and success. Admitting this to yourself might help you overcome the tendency to put off work and find out once and for all—both on and off the golf course—what you're really capable of accomplishing.

Time Management

THERE IS A SAYING THAT IF YOU REALLY WANT TO GET SOMETHING done, assign the task to an individual who has no time. Much as the rich keep getting richer, productive, well-organized people with exceptionally busy lives are the most likely people to find the time to take on one more responsibility.

Hazard Six individuals are notorious for their poor time-management skills. Always running late, miscalculating the time it will take to get a job done, life for these individuals is usually disorganized and harried. And what do you think is the reason that they don't stay with a new hobby, make it to the course early to hit balls, read books they have been meaning to get around to, or stick with an exercise program? Simple. It's because they don't have the time.

Hazard Six individuals have time all right. It's just that they are so consumed with the avoidance of failure or success, trying so hard to make their lives *easier,* that they typically find themselves spinning in circles, all the while believing that a disciplined life of working toward and accomplishing goals is just around the corner. Probably tomorrow or Monday, or at very worst, after the New Year. The problem with this logic is based on the simple truth that tomorrow never comes, that tomorrow's life is entirely too late.

Our society is currently inundated with time-management plans. Seminars, books, audiotapes, videotapes, computer programs, daily organizers, and so on. The stereotypic Hazard Six individual might recline in a Lazy-boy late at night, eating cold, leftover lasagna (not enough time to heat it up in the microwave), watching an infomercial for a set of tapes that promises to make the fortunate buyer more assertive, more confident, wealthier, and more organized in seven days . . . or your money back. And wouldn't it be just like this Hazard Six person to dial the toll-free number and put the product on a credit card—then, as a reward for finally taking some control over his or her life, grab a bowl of chocolate chip mint ice cream, a few Oreos, and a swig of milk, before heading off to bed.

I've said it before and I'll say it again. There are no quick fixes. If you want to stop swaying on your backswing, you will need to groove in hundreds, if not thousands of corrected swings, before it can be successfully and permanently altered. If you want to stop beating yourself up after a disappointing round of golf, you will have to restructure your distorted cognitions by exposure to multiple repetitions of rational thoughts. If you want to lose weight, rather than spend $800 on a new state-of-the-art treadmill, you might first consider consuming fewer calories than you burn. Successfully bringing about changes such as these is not unlike eating an elephant. And we all know that the only way to eat an elephant is one bite at a time.

In his book *How to Get Control of Your Time and Your Life*, author Alan Lakein suggests the "Swiss cheese" method for time management. He describes the method of "poking holes" in a large, seemingly overwhelming task by designating lots of small bits of time instead of waiting for that moment when you can get it all done at once. If, for instance, you have to wait for fifteen minutes while the oil is being changed in your car, use it toward the completion of some large-scale project, instead of sitting there daydreaming or speculating about the occupations of the other people in the waiting room. By breaking life into "little pieces," and taking advantage of "stolen moments," you will find that in much less time than you would have dreamed possible, you are accomplishing huge tasks that typically linger, fester, and agitate.

A little time each day results in the completed novel, the vegetable garden, the finished basement, the quilt, the fundamentally correct golf swing. The key is to understand how the process works. To know about Swiss cheese. Little pieces, lots and lots of little pieces, and anything can be accomplished.

For the Hazard Six individual, this awareness of and approach to the pursuit of tasks and dreams is a foreign concept. And even when the concept is comprehended, there still exists the tendency to sabotage the process. Fast out of the gate, Hazard Sixes tend to burn out early. Because it will take some time to explore and confront these issues, the best way to minimize the problem of self-destruction is to have a system for monitoring your behavior and your management of time.

Make Sure Someone Is Watching

REMEMBER HOW WHEN YOU WERE A KID AND YOU LIED ABOUT practicing a musical instrument or copied someone's homework, there was always a grownup around to tell you that you were only fooling yourself. As a kid I used to think, "Good enough, so long as I fooled everyone else and didn't get into any trouble." But as an adult, the logic doesn't hold up anymore. This fact is made perfectly clear on the golf course. Ever improve your angle to the green, around a tree, by swiping the ball with your foot? How did you feel? Cheating at golf can make you feel pretty down about an otherwise perfectly good round.

Whenever I feel the need to lose weight I go to a nutritionist. Actually, it doesn't have to be a nutritionist. Any kind of check-in program would do. Probably a phone booth manned by a derelict with a scale would suffice. But because I know myself, I know that I need something, someone to monitor my progress. Likewise, when I want to work on an area of my golf game, I take a lesson from a pro, make a commitment to practice, and schedule a follow-up lesson. Even though I'm an adult, there are some areas in my life where I still benefit from supervision.

Most people who come to me for counseling recognize that I do not have magic powers. What they are looking for is a safe place to disclose their thoughts and feelings, as well as for another human being to be aware of what it is they are setting out to accomplish. Of course, a person can commit to a goal and then cancel the next appointment. But there is less likelihood that they would break a commitment to me than there is that they would break a commitment to themselves. Stating aloud to another person that you are committed to work toward the accomplishment of a goal makes the probability of successful follow-through that much more likely.

Hazard Six individuals are very good at lying to themselves. This kind of self-deception usually takes the form of rationalization. In the case of Fred, when he hit that final drive and told himself that he was satisfied with his game as it was, he was rationalizing. For Fred to overcome the problem of being unable to persist at hard work and delay the gratification of feeling good, he would first have to admit to himself that he did in fact care very deeply about becoming a better golfer. Having accomplished some degree of self-honesty, he could then minimize the chances of falling prey to his self-defeating, rationalizing logic by committing to a goal-directed plan in the presence of another person. In Fred's case, a golf professional would probably make the most sense.

Write It Down

FOR THOSE OF YOU WHO ARE BEYOND THE STAGE OF LYING TO yourselves, who have clearly defined goals and a strong commitment to change, you probably can be entrusted with monitoring yourself. Self-monitoring can take many forms, but the most popular method is the use of a journal or more simply the listing of behaviors required to accomplish your goals. Journaling typically consists of writing down thoughts and feelings that you experience as you proceed through the stages of modifying your behavior. There are several advantages to keeping a diary, and many people do so even during times when they are not in the midst of a program of change. There is the advantage of "photographing your life," of avoiding the feeling that the days, months, and years of your life have become a blur. A second advantage of maintaining a journal is that it provides the opportunity to go back and see how you have grown, or how you handled situations in the past. A journal helps you maintain some sense of perspective in regard to where you are and where you have been.

The practice of writing down the behaviors required to reach your goals helps you avoid the tendency of lying to yourself. A good example comes from writing down a food plan for the purpose of dieting. If you only tell yourself that you'll make an effort to cut back, or to stop eating sweets, you probably won't. If you are serious about staying with a dietary food plan, you will write down exactly what foods you will eat, and if you are smart about it, you will designate weighed and measured portions.

I have a friend who is the antithesis of Hazard Six when it

comes to golf. In order to maintain his swing during the winter months, he installed a driving net in his garage. Each morning he rides his treadmill for forty-five minutes, during which time he reads golf improvement literature or watches a golf instructional video. Each evening he goes to his garage and takes a predetermined number of swings that focus on a single problem in fundamentals that he is trying to work out. Each day he writes down the details of his program, and has developed a system for recording the success of his endeavors. Once my friend overcomes his Hazard Five difficulties, and assuming that his wife and kids don't pack it in and leave, I believe that his program will eventually result in substantial game improvement. The point to be made is that the process of self-monitoring helps with focus and increases the probability of staying with a program for any form of self-improvement.

It's funny how writing down a goal heightens a sense of commitment and prevents the tendency for self-deception. Whenever my patients mention the desire to stop smoking, I ask them how much they smoke each day. Whether they tell me that their daily rate is five cigarettes or four packs, I can be certain that they have underestimated their smoking frequency. What do I do about it? I suggest that they hand-record each cigarette that they smoke. Not only are these individuals always surprised that they smoke as much as they do, but they usually begin to cut back immediately.

Even highly disciplined, successful individuals write down their goals. In an interview during the 1995 AT & T Pebble Beach Pro-Am, highly touted Tour rookie Justin Leonard was asked about his career goals. He replied that "I have those written down, but don't want to discuss them. Right now, I just want to keep on improving." The goal of simply improving is somewhat vague and difficult to define, but you can be certain that young Mr. Leonard has some very well-defined goals written down somewhere that only he knows about. This highly disciplined athlete will not risk leaving his highly motivated plan for growth and improvement to improvisation. Instead he has made a written contract with himself. By so doing, he stands an excellent chance of becoming a very prominent figure on the PGA Tour for many years to come.

9

Why People Resist Change

"They always say that time changes
things, but you actually have to change
them yourself."

—ANDY WARHOL

HOW MANY THERAPISTS DOES IT TAKE TO CHANGE A LIGHTBULB?
Only one . . . so long as the light bulb *really* wants to change. I
have heard that joke at more than one psychological conference
and have committed to getting up and leaving if I hear one more
keynote speaker recite it. But I begin this chapter with a stupid
joke that I have come to hate because it does succeed in making
a very good point.

A central question I repeatedly ask myself in the role of psychologist is: *Can people change?* I am not talking about temporary
changes such as a new diet or the beginning of an exercise program. And I am not talking about changes that occur as a result
of a crisis, such as illness or divorce, where an individual's life is
thrown so completely off its usual course that change is not so
much a decision as it is a necessary reaction to circumstance.
Rather, I am talking about substantial, meaningful, self-initiated
changes that happen not because you feel the heat, but because
you see the light. Changes that occur simply because you want
to be a different kind of person. Changes in basic qualities of
temperament not unlike the character traits represented by the
six Mental Hazards of Golf.

Do you believe in fate? That everything happens for a reason? That if something is meant to be, it is meant to be? The age-old question that philosophers have asked is whether man's existence is predetermined by forces outside of his control or whether he is basically free to live the kind of life he desires and be the kind of person he wishes to be. Are we bound to our genetic blueprint, forever forced to play the hand we were dealt? Or can we learn to be less of a worrier, more of a risk-taker, less moody, more assertive? The old nature-nurture question is another one of those "chicken-and-egg" issues that college students make sport of debating into the wee hours of the night. Issues that will never be resolved with definitive accuracy.

At this point in my life, I find that I am either too old, too tired, too bored, or too consumed with lowering my handicap to worry about these age-old existential debates that hallmarked my younger days. For this reason I have elected to adopt philosopher William James's designation of the human condition as being "half fated, half free." I figure that since we have no way of ever knowing for sure, why not split it down the middle. But this viewpoint still leaves one basic problem in need of resolution. If the half-free part is true, how does it happen? How can we take charge of the parts of our lives that we *are* free to change and successfully get rid of unwanted habits?

Changing and getting rid of unwanted habits is what this book is about, is what *all* self-help books are about. As I sit here and write a so-called self-help book, I find it somewhat awkward to confess that I have a problem with books that promise dramatic change simply because they have been read. Yet when I want to change some aspect of my behavior or personality, the first thing I do is run to the bookstore and devour any self-help material that is relevant to my area of concern. What makes self-help books useful for me is my understanding of *how* I can use them. I know that the words I read will find me in an already motivated state, willing to incorporate the reading material into a larger-scale program for change. And I have the advantage of realizing that there is no magic to be found in the written word. I have begrudgingly come to accept the reality that there is no magic to be found anywhere at all. Meaningful change does not occur in response to a single great moment of inspiration. Rather, change follows a predictable pattern that must be understood, accepted, and worked with if there is ever to be any forward movement.

The Nature of Change

YOU HAVE REACHED AN IMPORTANT MOMENT IN THIS BOOK. YOU have learned about the mental hazards that impede you in your everyday life and cause you to self-destruct on the golf course. You have been enlightened by the *MHAS* as to the specifics of your Mental Hazard Profile, and you have studied the techniques and ideologies that can help you to overcome your particular problem areas. Chances are you have identified with portions of the book and have felt inspired to utilize some of the suggestions. But if you are like most people, the inspiration will fade like sand filtering through a strainer and you will retreat back to old and familiar ways as quickly as you will forget your pledge to not yell at your children or to make sure to keep your backswing slow. This is how it goes with change. We resist it. Long-term habits are represented by deeply grooved, burned paths in our brains. We cannot help but slip back into the grooves that are so familiar and comfortable.

I had an opportunity to test the status of the positive change in my own mental hazard management just before I began this chapter. After writing anywhere from two to eight hours every day, for seventy-five straight days, I left for a Presidents' week family vacation in Florida. After some debate with myself and with my wife, I decided to leave the laptop behind. I decided that quality time with my family and getting away from the intellectual side of golf would be good for me. Playing golf instead of writing about it sounded like a very appealing prospect. I phoned ahead to arrange a few tee-times, feeling confident that I was in a good position to play well on the links of Orlando and Delray Beach. For one thing, my off-season fantasy golf game was always terrific. My winterized "mind swings" were pictures of Hoganesque perfection. Come February, I typically have the "swing" of Davis Love III (come June I'll be satisfied with President Clinton's) and the mental toughness of Corey Pavin (come September, Jack Lemmon's will do). Delusions aside, I had no doubt that all the time I put into the study of mental hazard management would serve me well when that moment arrived and I found myself once again standing over a golf ball for real.

I wasn't nervous about slotting in as a single at the Palms Course at Disney. Even when my miserable sense of direction resulted in an ill-advised last-minute arrival at the first tee, I managed to keep my emotions in check. I shook hands with Mike, the CPA from Jersey, who would share a cart with me that day, stretched, took a few gentle, then harder practice swings with my driver, took a cleansing breath, and did some differential relaxation before I stepped up and sent one 220 yards down the middle of the fairway. Bogey, par, par, double (can't get uptight about putting woes so early in the season), bogey, par. Four over after five holes on a tough and unfamiliar course after not swinging a club for three months was pretty darn good play for a bogey-at-best player like myself. Eighty degrees of sunny midwinter warmth, solid ball-striking, and the joy of recognizing in myself the conquest over Golf's Mental Hazards made for a darn near perfect day. I felt that I had done more than just "write the book." I finally learned how to live its message.

Before teeing off on 6, I remembered hearing that water came into play on 10 of the 18 holes of the Palms Course. At the time I hadn't given it a second thought, but after my tee shot on 6, water was all that I thought about. I know that five balls in the drink on one hole was my personal best but when my partner Mike mercifully insisted that I play my ball alongside his, as if I was lying 2, or when he recorded an 8 on the card (USGA rules designed to speed up play), I knew that I had managed to rack up a score of 15 on the par four 6th hole. And if my woes had ended there, I might have been able to live with it. What rattled my psyche was the fact that I did not strike a golf ball cleanly again for the rest of the day. And what infected my soul was the reappearance of the ugly feeling of worthless depression that stayed with me on the back nine. Had I brought it along, I might have been inclined to toss my Golf's Mental Hazards manuscript into the sparkling water hazard that rippled tauntingly in front of the green at 6.

Remember that bit from Chapter 5 about disappointment representing a potential opportunity? After two days of Hazard

Three despair, it hit me. Having just completed the family gig at Universal, I lay by the pool, replayed my swing in my mind, trying to make some sense out of what had happened. Suddenly, I woke up. Hazards Three and Five! Beginning with the tee shot in the water, I got too down on myself. By the time the hole was finished, I was deep into the despair mode of thinking. And that's when my old familiar nemesis Hazard Five kicked in. I lost faith in my swing, and was not letting go. My swing lost its fluidity as I tried to guide each and every shot. After two days of zero interest in picking up a golf club, I couldn't wait to get out again and focus on overcoming these two hazards. My opportunity came two days later when I took my 9-year-old son Adam to the par 60 Lakeview Golf Club in Delray Beach.

I know that an executive course does not generate the gut-check potential to be found on the big courses. But you still have to hit the ball and you still have to make some putts. No longer feeling down, my objective for the day was to forget about fundamentals and just trust my inner athlete to swing the club. I knew that destiny was on my side when I saw a newspaper clipping on the bulletin board in the pro shop. Lakeview was the course where the one-armed golfer, Sylvester "Cy" Young had his two holes in one.

At the day's end, I was once again in love with the glorious game of golf. I played the 18 holes in 8 over—9 bogeys, 8 pars, and 1 birdie. Adam—who demonstrates no difficulty whatsoever with Hazard Five—recorded his first ever birdie, on the third hole where I had my only birdie of the day. Father and son birdies, the recognition and overcoming of Golf's Mental Hazards, and more sunny skies made for a pretty great day. If I hadn't laid my bag on that red ant hill while we had 19th hole beverages, it could very well have been a perfect day.

I am back from Florida, again manning my computer station, feeling very good about the potential power of overcoming Golf's Mental Hazards. I believe that the five balls I hit into the water on the 6th hole at the Palms Course will be instrumental in helping me complete this book. For starters, it has helped me appreciate the significance of this chapter about change and the tendency people have to resist change, even when it is for the better. When the third and fifth hazards pervaded my thoughts and emotions, I regressed to a state that was very common during my earlier experiences as a golfer. Looking back on it now, it is hard for me to believe that I allowed myself to muddle in my negative mind-set for as long as I did. While still on the golf course, why was I incapable of recognizing what was happening to me? And why did it take two days of negative thinking and downtrodden moods before the light went on and I finally realized how ridiculously I was reacting?

As a psychologist, golfer, and human being, my life follows the same principles that govern the lives of every other struggling person on this planet. I can advise patients how to talk to their children, then go home and do exactly the opposite with my own. I can write about techniques for recognizing and recovering from Golf's Mental Hazards, and then go out and forget everything I know on the subject. I know that I have made substantial gains in the mental management of my golf game, but I also recognize the necessary sequence that *everyone* must go through during the process of changing long-term, undesirable habits.

The reason this chapter represents so critical a moment in this book is the same reason why an understanding of the nature of change is so central to any self-improvement endeavor. If left to live without self-analysis, effort, hard work, and risk-taking, most people would fall into a predictable, unalterable routine. No change is life's default mode. And the reality is that not everyone needs to change. If you have a decent life and a golf game that works for you, there is, of course, no need to rock the boat. But ask yourself honestly, are you satisfied with the conditions in your life? Do you want to explore buried parts of your personality, to experience more joy, less anxiety and depression, to at least become a better golfer? Depending on how you answer any of these questions, there are three basic options that you can follow. (1) Do your best to adapt to and accept the status quo, (2) live a life of "fast out of the gate, quick-fix" change programs that make a big splash but leave you in essentially the same place, or (3) accept life on life's terms and develop and commit to a program that is based on the realities inherent in the process of change.

The Compulsion to Repeat

SIGMUND FREUD COINED THE TERM "REPETITION COMPULSION" to describe the natural tendency for behaviors, thoughts, and feelings from our past to pull us back and eventually predominate. There are several theories that attempt to explain the phenomenon of the compulsion to repeat. Geneticists would say that we are doomed to live a preprogrammed life that is based on our genetic blueprint. Learning theorists would argue that familiar and repeating patterns of behavior are deeply programmed habits which are being repeated simply because they have been learned. I personally do not think that the *why* of the issue matters very much; just recognize that change is unnatural and that, without hard work and effort, life becomes a circle.

In current psychological jargon, the "comfort zone" is a term that is used to describe the phenomenon that draws individuals away from patterns of change, causing them to remain embedded in familiar and comfortable modes of behavior. It is based on the premise that we are most comfortable with behaviors that we have engaged in frequently in the past. Whenever we step out of routinized patterns we become *uncomfortable* and quickly retreat to what has worked for us in the past. A light and humorous yet practical and honest book called *Do It! Let's Get Off Our Buts* provides extensive discussion about the comfort zone. Authors John-Roger and Peter McWilliams state that "whenever we do something new, it falls outside the barrier of the comfort zone." The authors go so far as to suggest that "in even *contemplating* a new action, we feel fear, guilt, unworthiness, hurt feelings, anger—all those things we generally think of as 'uncomfortable.' "

Change is so unnatural and difficult to accomplish that Ken Blanchard, author of *Playing the Great Game of Golf* and president of the Golf University in San Diego, keeps "crying towels" on the range at his school. Recognizing the feelings of loss that his students will experience in response to any effort to change, the towels are designed "so people can cry and mourn the loss of old habits or ways of doing things that they might have liked but that are holding them back from getting better."

The essential point of this chapter, and to a great extent of this book, is that feelings we typically think of as uncomfortable are in fact the very feelings we need to work through and even embrace if there is to be any change for the better. And where is the discomfort of change any more apparent than with the game of golf? How many times have you taken a lesson and while the golf pro stands aside you strike the ball better than you have in recent memory. Perhaps the pro changed your grip, widened your stance, or told you to make a more complete turn on the backswing. And during the course of your lesson—while the pro was standing there with you and watching—you successfully made the change. Maybe the next day you went to the range and worked some more with this swing adjustment and continued to hit the ball well. You felt good about the swing change and more confident about your game in general.

Then comes the time to put your new swing to the *real* test— for instance, when you're playing against someone you really want to beat. Before the round, while at the range, you continue to employ your swing adjustment and continue to hit the ball well. You step between the tee markers for the first hole, and suddenly your entire perspective is dramatically different than it was during your lesson or at the range. And because golf will always be a game of frustration and misses, what do you think you will do the first time your game begins to suffer a bit? If you customarily slice the ball off the tee, it won't be long before you go back to the practice of aiming left of the fairway, allowing room for your old, familiar, and "comfortable" slice. Without even realizing it, you will retreat back to swing mechanics that have been grooved in over a period of years. On this particular day, the ways of the past might even work for you. You might play well and win your match. But once again, you have traded in the big picture for the moment by reverting to the "comfort" that you could spend a lifetime hoping to change.

The Role of Insight and Reeducation

CHANGE CAN BE BROKEN DOWN INTO TWO FUNDAMENTAL COMPOnents. The first is *insight*, or the understanding of what it is that you wish to change about yourself as well as what steps will be entailed in the process of attempting to alter the undesirable habit. The second is *reeducation,* or the actual changing of the behavior in question. Both steps are critical to the change process. Without insight, you would not understand which behaviors you wish to modify and could not possibly move along to the second step, the process of reeducation.

A very common illusion that many individuals in therapy have (many therapists believe it as well) is that, in and of itself, insight will produce change. *Aha . . . . I am intimidated by authority figures because my father was a critical and scholarly authoritarian.* What good is this information if it is not backed up with actual behavioral change? As a psychologist, I am always weary of the patient who has been to several therapists over the years and has read every self-help book in existence. Such individuals enjoy the intellectual stimulation of searching for the *whys* of their existence. Why am I so shy? Why do I defy authority? Why am I so self-conscious? Why? Why? Why? There is nothing wrong with intellectual curiosity and introspection. But if you don't study and practice the techniques that will help change your particular mental hazards, what have you accomplished?

How People Change is a short and brilliant book that realistically addresses the entire change process. The author, Dr. Allen Wheelis, states that "The place of insight is to illumine: to ascertain where one is, how one got there, how now to proceed, and to what end. It is a blueprint, as in building a house, and may be essential, but no one achieves a house by blueprints alone, no matter how accurate or detailed. A time comes when one must take up hammer and nails." Insight without follow-up action means that the house never gets built. And aside from being incomplete and ineffective, insight that is not acted upon can be extremely frustrating. How often have you thought to yourself, *I know exactly what my problems are. I just don't know how to go about changing them.* It can be argued that the individual stuck in the state of insight without action is worse off than the individual who does not even recognize that there is a problem. Not unlike being all dressed up with no place to go.

A Little Pain, Some Gain

BACK TO THE CRITICAL MOMENT IN THIS BOOK. YOU RECOGNIZE and accept the fact that certain mental hazards impede your golf game and perhaps your life outside of the golf course. Let's go so far as to say that you *really* want to change these hazardous qualities of temperament and that you are willing to do whatever it takes to accomplish this objective. Having established that change is a difficult and unnatural process, how do you begin to peck away at the seemingly overwhelming obstacles that stand between you and any hope for lasting self-improvement?

The following suggestions are essential components of the successful change process. Without incorporating these basic life principles into your self-improvement program, all that you've read to this point will evaporate and disappear into that dreaded place where all unrealized aspirations and dreams eventually wind up.

Get Back to Little Pieces. First of all, sit back, take a deep breath, and remind yourself that life is not a race against the clock. Many people are so afraid of not accomplishing enough in their lifetime that they try to do it all at once, and end up accomplishing nothing at all. Think of your life as a football game where you are down 21–0 in the first quarter. Do you have your quarterback start throwing bombs on every play? The successful team with the intelligent coach would not worry about the clock or the score. Rather, they would methodically employ a strategy that has had historical success. Establish the running game, throw in a couple of screen passes, and be satisfied if the drive results in a field goal. If you live your life as if you're double-parked, if you're throwing bombs on every play, you're not going to be successful at any long-term efforts for modifying unwanted habits or traits.

The concept of breaking life down into "little pieces" was presented in regard to the Hazard Six golfer. This is no coincidence since Hazard Six individuals are inherently misguided about the realistic process of successful change. But everyone struggles with change to one degree or another. And nobody enjoys the necessary pain that is a by-product of the frustration, regression, and generally slow pace of meaningful change. Regardless of whether your life and your golf game are impeded by any or all of the six Mental Hazards, one factor does not change: the enormous advantage of being able to focus on the moment at hand, on the "little piece" that you are facing right now.

Where is your life today? Are you unhappy with your job? Angry at your spouse or one of your kids? Tired of three-putting? Rather than quit your job, have an affair, or buy a new putter, how about making one simple decision. Talk to a supervisor or co-worker, or update your resume. Maybe you need to plan a weekend away alone with your partner or to take your kid to a movie. Or how about buying a rollaway putting green and committing to practice putting for twenty minutes a day, five days a week? Whatever problem you face, remember that it *is* solvable. *Every* problem can *always* be solved. It just probably won't happen today or, for that matter, tomorrow or the next day.

Break the problem down into little pieces, into lots of little problems. And then take your own sweet time. The "no pain, no gain" mentality of the 1990s has a certain degree of merit and validity. But it doesn't have to be as "black and white" as is depicted in athletic footwear commercials. You can buy the sneakers and you can run eight miles a day, but you still won't be Jerry Rice or Shaquille O'Neil. Better off running a mile a day, gratified and secure in the knowledge that you are on the right track for problem-solving and lasting change.

The Process Works If You Want It To. Not unlike a lot of high-handicap golfers, I have a tendency to swing from over the top. Two seasons ago, I decided to finally stop doing so. I scheduled a lesson with Tom, my personal swing doctor, and voiced my commitment to once and for all put an end to this problem. At the range, Tom placed two tees in the ground. One to my right—depicting the inside path the club should take on the backswing—and one in a direction to the right of the target area. This technique helped me enormously during the lesson. Not only was I swinging inside-out, but I was actually hitting the ball with a little draw as opposed to my usual fade if not slice. I was thrilled. The simplicity in Tom's placement of the two tees was brilliant. I made a decision to use the two-tee technique every time I went to the range from that day on.

I honestly don't remember what happened after that lesson. I used the placed tees at the range a few times, but I don't have any recollection of hitting the ball with a draw again. And when I was tired, frustrated, or just not into my game, I continued to come over the top. Still do. Where did my enthusiasm go? What happened to my motivation to change my swing plane? As I look back at it today, I realize that I ignored the most valuable part of my lesson with Tom—the part when he told me that in order to change the path of my swing, to have it become entrenched in my motor memory, I would have to repeat the proper swing thousands of times. It's not that I didn't believe him, it's just that I didn't stay with the program. I gave up in response to the frustration of not being readily able to transfer my swing at the range to my swing on the course.

According to Chuck Hogan, author of *Five Days to Golfing Excellence*, and president of Sports Enhancement Associates, a swing change must be practiced 60 times a day for 21 consecutive days if it is to become part of a newly structured motor memory. In addition, each and every practice swing during the learning phase must be given 100 percent attention. I definitely believe that Mr. Hogan knows what he is talking about. I also know that I have never practiced with the kind of commitment he is suggesting as being necessary for actual change. Is it any wonder I still come over the top more often than I would care to admit?

There is a process for change that works. It is based on proper technique along with a necessary number of repetitions. The Hazard One golfer cannot practice self-hypnosis once, twice, or even three times and expect to be free from anxiety on the first tee. The Hazard Three golfer can restructure his or her cognitions ten, maybe fifty times and still not avoid getting down after substandard play. Mental factors cannot be broken down as definitively as motor skills. I cannot provide you with the specific timeframe or number of repetitions necessary to overcome mental hazards in the same manner that Chuck Hogan could for swing mechanics.

But despite the differences in physical versus psychological change, the basic principles of the change process are identical. They both require insight into what it is that needs to be changed, a technique for bringing this change about, and lots and lots of repetitions of this technique. Follow this formula and it will eventually work for you, unless, of course, the one final and essential ingredient is missing—that being the motivation to make the change, the motivation and the willingness to endure the frustration and setbacks that are a fact of life in the process of changing old behaviors. How many therapists does it take to change a lightbulb? How many golf pros does it take to change one golfer's over-the-top swing? It all comes down to desire. You know what you need to do. And if it doesn't happen for you, the only plausible explanation is that you don't want it enough.

Don't Forget Your Mental Hazard Profile. I guess it's not surprising that as a professional psychologist and amateur golfer, I am more committed to changes that impact on my personal life and emotions than I am to changes in my golf game. It's not that I don't want to be a better golfer, it's just that I recognize my anatomical and athletic limitations. I really don't expect to be regularly shooting in the 70s during this lifetime. But mental management is a different matter entirely. For one thing it impacts on my every waking moment, not just during those times when I am playing golf. And I still maintain the belief that learning to overcome Golf's Mental Hazards *will* lower my handicap in addition to providing me with a more gratifying, productive, and self-accepting life.

One positive aspect of the compulsion to repeat past behaviors is that it provides a method for self-diagnosis. For instance, if you are having a tough round of golf that you believe is based on mental factors, and you know that you typically struggle with Hazards Two and Five, you can figure that these same problem areas are again responsible for the self-destruction of your golf game. The same principle applies to swing mechanics. How many times do you have to remind yourself to keep your head still or to take the club back slowly before you stop repeating the same basic mistake in technique? The answer is that you will never entirely solve the problem. People are not machines and are not capable of perfection when it comes to the replication of feelings, thoughts, or behaviors. That's why even professional golfers have days when their swings are not in sync. The advantage they have over the recreational golfer is based on their acceptance of performance fluctuation along with a system for diagnosing what the problem might be.

After my disappointing round in Orlando, it took me two days before I realized that my problems were rooted in Hazards Three and Five. I should have known that my problem could be found in these self-destructive qualities because I know myself and I know that getting discouraged and trying to control the flight of the golf ball have been my predominant mental liabilities since I first picked up a 7-iron. But after a disappointing round, emotions become blurred and confused in a manner that makes any chance at objective self-analysis impossible. Even for an insightful and educated psychologist like myself, it is inevitable that I become lost in myself, that I buy into my self-doubting state of confusion for a while. Why this is the case, I cannot say for sure. Perhaps it is part of Freud's "repetition compulsion," just a piece of human nature.

But I have grown substantially as a "mental golfer." A few years back, I would have lived with the self-doubt for weeks, for months, never really understanding my problem, rather just waiting for it to quietly lift and disappear from sight. When I became aware of the reasons for my disappointing round, it was no coincidence that I happened to be thinking at the time about the various Mental Hazards of Golf. And I believe that this method for self-analysis is what has made the difference in the mental management of my game. I now have a structured set of factors to review and analyze. I have an awareness of my Mental Hazard Profile. And when I struggle the next time, I will know where to go for the solution to my confusion and despair. Granted, it might take a day or two before I "wake up" and even remember to look for the answers to my golfing woes. But remember that Curtis Strange is capable of forgetting to breathe properly during an important round, and with the best intentions, you very well might forget to not yell at the kids, or to bring the club back low and slow.

You know which of Golf's Mental Hazards tend to give you difficulty. If you're struggling with your game, probably the same ones again are responsible. A big advantage of the compulsion to repeat is that the past continues to be the best guide in the present and predictor of the future. If you're not playing as well as you know you could, study your Mental Hazard Profile. Pick out the hazards that are in the elevated range, and read the corresponding chapters once again. Listen carefully to the words as you read them and practice the techniques with regularity and attentiveness. Do the same the next time you struggle, and the time after that, and the multitude of times that inevitably will follow. If you diagnose and recover with greater rapidity over the months and years, then you have made as substantial a change as is humanly possible. And who can say for certain that you won't beat the odds and someday manage to permanently fix a mental flaw in your attitude or a physical flaw in your golf swing. Freudian theory would predict it to be impossible. It would predict that you will be compelled to repeat old ways again and again. But then again, the father of psychology just might be wrong. Let's face it . . . Sigmund Freud wasn't known for his golf game.

10

In The Zone

"As I watched the seagulls, I thought,
That's the road to take; find the absolute
rhythm and follow it with absolute trust."

—NIKOS KAZANTZAKIS

IT DOESN'T HIT YOU UNTIL AFTER YOUR ROUND IS OVER. WITH NO particular swing thoughts in mind, no concern about technical details, no worry, no frustration, it all went your way on this particular day. Looking back, you recognize that the round played out slowly yet time flew by. Every detail of every moment was crystal clear to you. Instinctively, without need for analysis, without even thinking—so it now seems—you knew how to play each shot. You walked up confidently to each tee and looked out at huge, expansive fairways that contained generous landing areas for your strong, accurate drives. Your putting stroke was fluid, never tentative, and you recall several instances where you *knew* that a putt was going in even before you prepared to stroke it. What did you do differently on this day? You know you played far better than you had any right to play, and now that the round is over, you can't help but wonder why. Now that the round is over, you have—for the first time all day—finally waked up and realized all the usual ways to screw up a golf round that you somehow avoided on this day. You know that if your current awareness had occurred at any point while you were still playing, it would have all ended right there. By waking up and becoming conscious of what it is that you were doing, the magic would have picked up and disappeared.

All sports refer to moments of "out of your mind" peak performance as being in "The Zone." No sport seems to bear the potential of going in and out of this state like golf does. It could have been Michael Jordan hitting nine out of ten jumpers or Roger Clemens using twenty pitches to strike out six consecutive batters, but these were atypical moments of spectacular peak performances that were not necessarily essential for victory in their respective sports. Watch a PGA tournament on any given weekend, however, and the man being chased by the pack is typically in that mystical place. And it's not only professional golfers who get to experience the magic. Any hacker who puts his time in gets to visit The Zone every now and then.

Sports psychologists have made careful study of the physical and psychological factors that are a part of Zoned-in play. Despite great progress in this area of research, one fact remains undisputed: The Zone cannot be entirely controlled or accessed at will. Although there is a clear-cut set of factors involving preparation and mental management during actual play that increase the likelihood of finding The Zone, there still comes a time when the golfer must simply and matter-of-factly wait. The groundwork can be done, and the professional golfer could know that he has put himself in the optimal position to most probably be the beneficiary of the "Zone Gods." But even at this point, it is often necessary to wait. To wait until the time is right and it is your turn to be graced by the powers that be.

The objective of this chapter is to teach you how to increase the frequency of your visits to The Zone. Much of this has already been covered in the previous sections of this text, for Zoned-in play is Hazard-free play. If you're struggling with the autonomic symptoms of anxiety or anger, if you're getting too high after a great shot, or too down after a disappointing moment, if you are expending energy with the concern about others' impressions of your golf performance, or remain supplanted in the struggle to control the flight of your golf shots, and of course, if you are unwilling to put the time into your game, the preconditions for finding The Zone are far less than optimal. If you still need considerable work on one or more of Golf's Mental Hazards, you have failed the prerequisite for deriving much benefit from this chapter. For the methods of creating the optimal set of preconditions for The Zone constitute very advanced material that will only benefit those who have mastered the rudiments of solid mental play.

If you find yourself still at the level of introductory student, no need to despair. You will still have your moments in The Zone just by stepping out there often enough. But they will be few and far between. For those of you ready to move on to the next level, please be advised that you will continue to have a substantial number of golfing experiences that are commonplace and ordinary, if not occasionally dreadful and ugly. But you will be among the few who are in a position to sit back, anticipate, and wait, for you will have put your time in, completed all the groundwork known to modern science, and all that will remain will be the ability to be patient. And while you wait for a visit to The Zone, be grateful for having the awareness and self-discipline to be in the position you are in and for the knowledge that whether it comes today, tomorrow, in three weeks, or in a month, you will again experience the joy and the magic.

What It's Like in "The Zone"

AL GEIBERGER'S AND CHIP BECK'S ROUNDS OF 59 MUST BE RANKED among the most famous instances of play in The Zone in PGA history. During the 1977 Memphis Classic, where Al Geiberger became the first PGA player to break 60 during tournament play, he was quoted as saying, "I didn't realize at the moment exactly what I had done . . . I only realized the enormity of it when I walked into the press room and got a long, standing ovation. It wasn't until I came out of my daze that I began to appreciate my accomplishment."

U.S. Amateur champion Tiger Woods detailed during an interview with *The New York Times Magazine* that his manner of accessing The Zone is by keeping his conscious mind out of his play. "You ever go up to a tee and say, 'Don't hit it left, don't hit it right'?" he questioned his interviewer. "That's your conscious mind. My body knows how to play golf. I've trained it to do that. It's just a matter of keeping my conscious mind out of it."

The comments of Al Geiberger and Tiger Woods both point toward an unconscious, "no-brain" quality that occurs with Zoned-in play. And even most high-handicappers would agree with this assessment. You can take lessons, learn the fundamentals, and work hard on developing these skills; but there must come a moment when you stop learning golf and thinking about what you have learned and simply play golf. Needless to say, Tiger Woods's body knows how to play golf because he has enormous innate athletic ability and has been swinging a club every day since early in his childhood. He can well afford to let go of his conscious mind and trust his body to play a superior brand of golf. But can you, a far more average golfer, also consider learning to trust *your* inner athlete, complete with its reverse pivot, misaligned swing plane, and less than ideal eye-hand coordination?

The answer is an unequivocal yes. Your goal is not to play as well as a professional or, for that matter, an amateur phenom. Your goal is to play to the best of *your* capabilities. If you have an 18 handicap and spend a round in The Zone, it is most likely that you will score in the low 80s, a score that would constitute a horrible performance for a professional golfer. But on your day in The Zone, what you experienced was highly similar to what Al Geiberger, Chip Beck, or Tiger Woods experienced when he visited that same place. The Zone does not know handicaps. Play in The Zone is not about a score, but rather about a state of consciousness, a place the mind of mortals can visit for short periods of time. And all golfers—from Ben Hogan to Jack Nicklaus to you and me—are merely mortals. We might not have the ability to play golf as well as they do, but we can *feel* just as they do when on top of our games.

Charles A. Garfield, the author of *Peak Performance: Mental Training Techniques of the World's Greatest Athletes*, talked extensively with accomplished athletes about the way it felt to perform in The Zone. As a result of these interviews, he developed a list of eight physical and psychological correlates of peak performance. They are

1. *Mentally relaxed*—The athletes felt calm and highly focused. Their ability to concentrate was unusually sharp.

2. *Physically relaxed*—The athletes reported feeling limber and loose.
3. *Confident and optimistic*—The athletes believed beforehand that they would perform well.
4. *Focused on the present*—The athletes were "process" as opposed to "product oriented." In golfing terms, they were totally into the shot at hand, not thinking about past or future performance.
5. *Highly energized*—The athletes felt "pumped," ready and eager to take on the physical demands required of their sport.
6. *Extraordinary awareness*—The athletes felt very much in tune with the way their bodies felt as well as with details of the environment.
7. *In control*—Although the athletes reported being *in control*, they recognized a sense of not forcing matters, of letting things happen.
8. *In the "cocoon"*—The athletes felt as though in a "bubble." They were aware of everything around them, but found it impossible to be distracted.

You might notice the relationship between the above-stated conditions of Zoned-in play and the objectives of overcoming Golf's Mental Hazards. The purpose for learning about your Mental Hazard Profile, as well as for studying methods that can facilitate the overcoming of these self-destructive qualities, is to improve your golf and to make it more consistent. A bonus that comes along with this higher degree of consistency is more frequent visits to The Zone.

A point that has been repeated throughout this book is that people—even great athletes—are far from perfect, and accordingly will experience performance fluctuations now and forever. Players like Bobby Jones, Ben Hogan, and Jack Nicklaus had more success in consistently managing their mental skills and experiencing Zoned-in episodes of play than most other golfers in the course of history. And it's not to say that these men had better physical skills than their peers during their respective runs of greatness. The PGA Tour, particularly today, is loaded with enormously talented players with prettier swings and more impressive ball-striking abilities than the greatest of all time. What they don't have is the consistency of the greats. And who can blame them. For even the professional Tour golfer has a life. A life filled with the problems of career, family, fears, and insecurities. Of dealing with the daily details of making a living, catching an airplane, making the cut, making contact with a disgruntled child or spouse, a swing change, a hotel change, a twinge in the lower back, an unexplained feeling of sadness or emptiness. How the greats can consistently block out the everyday details of the mortal existence and find The Zone is an amazing accomplishment.

I know that at times I am incapable of clearing my mind of miscellaneous sources of stress and focusing on the game of golf. There are days when, despite all my knowledge about technique and theory, I simply cannot apply what I know to the matter of finding a fluid swing and hitting a golf ball with accuracy and authority. And although a Ben Hogan or a Jack Nicklaus—complete with ideal body and mind for handling the demands of golf—comes along twice a century or so, I figure that most of you are more like me than you are like the greats. I love my occasional visits to The Zone and continue to invest myself in the pursuit of having a greater number of opportunities to experience the wonderful feeling of mindless escape. My plan, outlined in the remaining portions of this chapter, has already begun to yield successful results.

Even One Hazard Is Too Many

IF YOU STUDY THE CHARACTERISTICS THAT DEFINE ZONED-IN PLAY, it becomes clear that any one of the hazards can effectively ruin your chance for a peak performance. You know which hazards give you the most trouble. How hard have you worked on overcoming these problem areas? Without such an investment of time and effort, visits to The Zone will be left to occur during those instances that are the exception rather than the rule, on those days when for some reason you are *not* in your usual state of discomfort and low self-confidence. It might very well be true that access to The Zone cannot be entirely controlled by any mere mortal, but if you haven't made a serious effort to overcome *your* mental hazards, you have ignored a substantial piece that is very well within your control.

A quick review of each of the six Mental Hazards of Golf will demonstrate why the presence of even one mental hazard is one too many to allow a visit to The Zone.

HAZARD	IMPACT ON THE ZONE	ANTIDOTES
One: *The fear of fear*	Mental and physical tension Low confidence Low energy Poor concentration and awareness	Cleansing breaths Relaxation Positive self-talk Self-hypnosis Experience situations that make you nervous
Two: *Losing your cool*	Mental and physical tension Low confidence Hyperaroused Unfocused	Cleansing breaths Relaxation Positive self-talk Self-hypnosis Examine issues of low self-esteem
Three: *Getting too up or too down*	Low confidence Low energy Poor concentration and awareness	Restructure cognitive distortions Take one shot at a time Be proactive; have a plan Examine issues of low self-esteem
Four: *Worrying what others think*	Mental and physical tension Low confidence Hyperaroused Poor concentration and awareness	Cleansing breaths Relaxation Positive self-talk Self-hypnosis Remember that nobody cares and that nobody is perfect Confront situations that make you self-conscious
Five: *The need to be in control*	Mental and physical tension Low confidence	Use both sides of your brain Use a trigger

	Poor concentration and awareness	Develop a preshot routine
	Freezing up	Use only one swing thought
Six: *An unwillingness to work*	Low confidence	Examine issues of low self-esteem
	Poor concentration and awareness	Improve management of time
		Have someone monitor your progress

The more time you put into overcoming Golf's Mental Hazards, the more trips you will take to The Zone. And once you feel that you have done all you can do in this regard, that you have substantially improved the management of your mental skills, there is another body of information that can further facilitate peak performance. This information, the essence of which remains outside the confines of scientific awareness, can only be partially comprehended. It is about secrets and subconscious wishes, about mystery and magic. It is that portion of The Zone for which we have no rational explanations.

The Other Side of Life

OVER THE PAST SEVERAL YEARS, THERE HAS BEEN A SUBSTANTIAL movement toward an acknowledgment of powerful and invisible forces that represent the part of ourselves that we cannot understand or access and thus tend to deny. Call it the spirit, the subconscious, or the soul, our culture has become fascinated with the examination of this portion of our inner selves. One need look no further than the best-seller list to see evidence of this dramatic shift in thinking.

James Redfield, author of the best-selling novel *The Celestine Prophecy*, makes a strong case for a transcendent, spiritual move toward finding meaning in the seemingly chance events that compose our daily lives. Prior to embarking on an adventure to find a manuscript containing the Nine Insights which will shed light on this spiritual awakening, a character in Redfield's story named Charlene informs the main character that, "We are sensing again, as in childhood, that there is another side of life that we have yet to discover, some other process operating behind the scenes."

The seemingly simple game of golf has a strong foothold in this "other side of life." And never is this more apparent than in moments of Zoned-in play. Haven't you ever felt the presence of a force beyond your own ability and willfulness that allowed an impossible putt to stumble upon the hole? Have you not had days when tee to green, you were possessed, if not by a spiritual force, by the ghost of some unfamiliar golfer? A golfer with an effortless feel for the game along with a handicap very much lower than your own?

You can study the fundamentals of the golf swing, you can learn to overcome all of Golf's Mental Hazards, and you will no doubt be a much improved golfer. But the circle will remain unclosed, the gap representing forces that mysteriously come and go and can only be experienced, never entirely understood. To close this gap requires more than understanding and hard work. The circle can only be closed with a "leap of faith" into the unknown place where body meets mind and mind intuitively connects with the invisible forces that govern all things.

Remember the scene in the movie *Caddyshack*, where Chevy Chase's character, Mr. Webb, tells young caddie Danny Noonan that "There is a force in the universe that makes things happen. And all you have to do is get in touch with it. Stop thinking, let things happen, and *be the ball.*" Recall the moment in Michael Murphy's *Golf in the Kingdom* when Shivas Iron accomplished the feat of "oneness with the ball" and of letting things happen, when he registered his midnight hole-in-one with a shillelagh at the 13th hole at Burningbush—a moment that stands alone in literature as the single most intense example of Zoned-in play.

Twenty-five years after *Golf in the Kingdom* was published, Michael Murphy finds interest in the spiritual side of golf to be stronger than ever. During an interview with *Golf* magazine, Murphy discussed the recent trend of PGA Tour professionals to acknowledge the magic: "Here were people playing this game at its highest level who knew exactly what I was talking about— that something extraordinary can happen when you're playing golf, especially when you play at your peak. By that I mean you don't seem to swing the golf club. It swings you. Some call it 'The Zone,' a moment when body and soul seem to function in a state of almost unconscious bliss. All athletes experience it, but golf seems to possess a unique genius for bringing this out."

In the wonderful golf fantasy novel, *The Legend of Bagger Vance*, author Steven Pressfield introduces the character of Bagger Vance, the caddie and mentor to an amateur engaged in a mythical 36-hole golf match against Bobby Jones and Walter Hagen. Set in the deep South in 1931, Vance guides his pupil, Junah, through the match and toward his "Authentic Swing." More than just a solid golf swing, the Authentic Swing is a smaller part of a meaningful and Authentic Life. In an effort to help his student draw from the spirit and energy of his world-class competitors, Vance offers Junah the following words of wisdom: "Hagen and Jones do not will the swing into being, they use their will to 'find' the swing that is already there, that was there before they were born and will continue to exist through eternity. Then they will surrender their will to it."

Golfers who have visited The Zone believe in the wisdom of Shivas Irons and Bagger Vance. The estimate that 35 million people will be playing golf by the end of this decade is testimony to the fact that more and more, people are looking beyond the material orientation of the 1980s with an eye on greater comfort with self, a heightened sense of meaningfulness and enlightenment, which of course means more pars. Although much of the time spent on a golf course is filled with predictable, highly ordinary experiences, the seductive lure of those visits to The Zone keeps the golfer coming back for more. Once a golfer has experienced the timeless, effortless, childlike magic of Zoned-in play, it is impossible to remain unaffected. The golfer knows that he has stumbled upon some dark, deep secret that is not just about hitting a golf ball straight and long. He knows that he has accessed a part of himself that lies outside the commonplace, daily world of ego-driven material pursuits and athletic conquests. After a visit to The Zone, the golfer is a kid again, complete with a belief in magic and the confidence that anything is possible.

The Zone and Zen

VISITS TO THE ZONE HAVE MUCH IN COMMON WITH THE IDEALS and goals of Zen Bhuddism. In Zen, the objective is to attain a "beginner's mind." During this state, the individual exists only in the present moment, with no preconceived notions, no expectations, no thoughts at all. Beginner's mind remains ready to experience whatever passes before it. It is unbiased and open to all possibilities.

The study of Zen is centuries old and applies to each and every earthly experience, not just holes-in-one or greens in regulation. It is possible to be in a Zen-like Zone during any of life's activities. Have you ever become totally absorbed in material you were reading, listened to each and every word spoken to you by a young child, focused on your activated taste buds while eating a chocolate ice cream cone? These moments of pure and uncompromised focus typify the beginner's mind that is the basic objective of the practice of Zen. I believe that golf played in The Zone approximates this mind-set.

Through long-term devotion to the practice of *zazen*—a "lotus position," meditative exercise—students of Zen work toward the goal of accomplishing the unbiased clarity of beginner's mind. As a hyperactive, red-meat-eating, neurotic worrier (with a mild case of scoliosis), it is not my intention to convert you to the practice of sitting cross-legged and straight-spined in the hopes of becoming one with the universe. But there are elements in the process of overcoming Golf's Mental Hazards that do, in fact, share much in common with the principles of Zen.

The fear, rage, moodiness, and self-consciousness that depict Hazards One through Four all run counter to the "no-brain," mindlessness that is at the heart of Zen theory and characterizes play in The Zone. The techniques of proper breathing, physical relaxation, and self-hypnosis, which were presented for the purpose of overcoming these hazards, create bodily states highly similar to those accomplished during the practice of *zazen*. The work ethic prescribed for Hazard Six sufferers is a necessary part of the Zen student's quest for beginner's mind. Likewise, it is no coincidence that golfers who invest time and effort into their game experience a greater frequency of Zoned-in play.

It is confronting Hazard Five, however, that I believe to be most central to the Zen-like mind-set that is critical for play in The Zone. The need to be in control is probably the one hazard that *everyone* struggles with to one extent or another. Understanding the paradox of making things happen by not trying to make them happen is a critical requirement of the Zen state of beginner's mind and for visits to The Zone. The ability to translate this understanding to the physical side of golf might be easier said than done, but there are tools designed to enable this possibility.

If it is true that Hazard Five represents the critical obstruction to The Zone, it would follow that the practice of using a trigger along with a consistent preshot routine would facilitate instances of Zoned-in play. Perhaps this is exactly why *all* pro golfers employ both of these techniques before each and every shot. The world's greatest golfers might have overcome the other Mental Hazards of Golf, but they recognize that there will always remain forces that are unclear if not invisible that they simply cannot control. Call it the subconscious, call it God, but know that a force greater than yourself is busy at work, determining the outcome of your golf round and of your life. The regimen of a preshot routine and of a trigger is testimony to this Higher Power. It is the golfer's way of acknowledging that certain repeated practices allow for enhanced mindless play despite variations in circumstance. It is the best way for the golfer to get in the way of forces that enter and pass through body and mind, en route to journeys into The Zone.

Another critical component of Zoned-in play that is central to the principles of Zen is the ability to concentrate. After superhuman rounds, golfers will often talk about how the world around them seemed to play out in slow-motion. How there was time to process every factor of every shot, how they could see the clubhead strike the ball and at the same time notice the sound of a crow, how there was plenty of time to calmly sort out details and at the same time enjoy the camaraderie of playing partners or the vision of picturesque moments. Consider the alternative, when you smack ball after ball with little sense of purpose, until exiting the course with an escalated score, an achy body, and an uncomfortably distorted and confused recall of the round's details. Some individuals are definitely more adept at concentrating than others, but concentration is a Zen and a Zone-related skill that is at least partially understood by Western culture. It is a skill that can be practiced and improved upon.

Developing Concentration Skills

I'M THE KIND OF PERSON WHO ONLY PAYS ATTENTION TO SOMEthing when I am totally interested in it. I am what psychologists might call "highly distractible." It is not at all uncommon for me to read several pages in a book before suddenly realizing that I have no clue about what I have been reading (wake up!). By forgetting to look for my exit on a highway, I've been known to travel from Albany to New York City via scenic routes such as Vermont or Massachusetts. If I don't carefully follow a movie in the early stages (particularly Tom Clancy movies), you might as well stick a fork in me . . . . I'm done.

Aside from wasting time and occasionally embarrassing myself, my poor concentration skills never created any substantial problems for me. That is, until I began to play golf. There are so many distractions on a golf course—people, scenery, thoughts about anything and everything—that I find it extremely difficult to lock into the ball (let alone be the ball) for shot after shot, hole after hole. Even Jack Nicklaus agrees. Despite admitting to being "blessed with the ability to focus intensely on whatever I'm doing through most distractions, and usually to the exclusion of whatever else might otherwise preoccupy me," Nicklaus concedes that he "still can't concentrate on nothing but golf shots for the time it takes to play 18 holes."

Turn It On and Off. You've got to figure that if Jack Nicklaus can't concentrate for four or five hours, not many other golfers will even come close. For this reason, the first rule of effective concentration for golf has to do with learning how to turn it on and turn it off. Nicklaus refers to his particular regimen as one "that allows me to move from peaks of concentration into valleys of relaxation and back again as necessary." As soon as he completes a successful shot, Nicklaus allows himself to descend into one of his relaxed valleys. He does so "either through casual conversation with a fellow competitor or by letting my mind dwell on whatever happens into it."

One problem that I tend to experience on the golf course is that I sometimes get lost in a valley. I love to let my mind wander and I enjoy socializing, and there have been many occasions where I have suddenly found myself standing over a golf ball, ill-prepared to hit it. For a while, I went to the other extreme and focused so intensely on each and every shot that I lost out on the pleasure of my surroundings and the company of my playing partners. There is nothing wrong with becoming entirely immersed in your game, so long as you find this to be pleasurable. During occasional rounds, I enjoy getting lost in myself, remaining quiet, focusing only on my game. But a steady dose of intense, bear-down golf would remove for me so much of what I enjoy about the game. So long as you know yourself, and develop a method for stepping in and out of states of concentration, you will be in a good position to maintain an adequate level of focus throughout a golf round.

Be Target-Oriented. Picking your spots for intensive concentration is not enough if you do not understand *how* to concentrate. I remember playing with a friend who proclaimed before the round that he was going to bear down on every shot and make it a point to not lose a single stroke to a failure to concentrate. This friend got off to a poor start which quickly degenerated to a state of downright ugliness. It was frustrating yet comical to see this man stand over his ball, gritting his teeth, staring a hole into it. He believed that concentration and focus were about intensity. Intensity is okay when it is properly guided. This friend obviously had no clue about how to harness his intensity. He had no idea as to *how* to concentrate.

Dr. Fran Pirozzolo, chief of Neuropsychology Services at the Baylor College of Medicine, defines concentration as "the narrowing of attention," adding that the professional golfer fixes attention on the target while the high-handicapper focuses on either mechanics, hitting the ball hard, or landing areas such as trees or sands that he hopes to avoid. Dr. Pirozzolo suggests becoming more target-oriented like the pro. To accomplish this objective, it is recommended that the golfer imagine a huge archery target just a few feet away. Then "concentrate intently on the image for a few seconds, seeing your ball smashing right through its center."

Nick Price agrees with the notion that being target-oriented is essential for the level of concentration required for play in The Zone. "The more I focus, the less I worry about pressure and everything else. My mind is totally and completely into the target. Some people choose to worry about hitting out-of-bounds, some choose to think about their swing, but when I'm looking down at the ball, I actually see the target."

Target-orientation is an advanced skill that requires well-developed motor memory (which means lots of practice) as well as a special ability to block out extraneous thoughts, sights, and sounds. Taken to an extreme, target-orientation brings us back to the Zen-like magic of "being the ball," or as stated in Eugen Herrigel's *Zen in the Art of Archery*, "the archer aiming at himself —and yet not at himself, in hitting himself—and yet not himself, and thus becoming simultaneously the aimer and the aim, the hitter and the hit."

For those of you who have enough trouble hitting the ball, let alone being the ball, suffice it to say that you need to at least be aware of the target, or where you wish the ball to land, on each and every shot. Keep in mind that the target is not necessarily represented by the flagstick. Off the tee, you need to pick out a piece of fairway and designate that as your target. And notice that I said a piece of fairway. Zen master or not, you do not want to make the beginner's mistake of thinking in terms of an antitarget, or a place that you do not want your ball to end up. That's how the golf architects make their money and get their jollies. They know that the average golfer will be hitting away from a trap, water hazard, or wooded out-of-bounds area. Don't take the bait. Think only about where you want your ball to go, not about areas that you hope and pray to avoid.

If You Have More On Your Mind Than the Target. What do you typically think about when you stand over the ball? I know that I still tend to focus too much on some swing thought that pertains to mechanics such as full shoulder turn, low and slow, or to throw my hands at the target. If you are a relative newcomer to the game or working on some change in your swing, a focus on mechanics is necessary until you have grooved the proper swing and successfully etched it into your motor memory. Just recognize that it is not an effective way to play well and ideally find a Zoned-in level of play.

If your swing is mechanically flawed, make a decision. Are you willing to put the time, effort, and expense into improving your swing? If so, find a pro that you feel comfortable with, and plan on investing a good deal of time in practice. When you do go out to play, never attempt to work with more than *one* swing thought. Before the round, try a couple of swing thoughts at the practice range, find one that works, and commit to it for the entire round. Your swing will inevitably regress at least partially back to old form during the course of the round. It will then be time to get back to the range and methodically go about the business of grooving in that new swing.

When you're out on the course, make every effort to get away from mechanics and concentrate on a *whole fluid swing*. When in The Zone, your inner sense of rhythm and flow is operating instinctively, unimpeded by thoughts about proper swing path, clubhead position, or the wrist cock. The swing happens far too quickly for mechanical thoughts to serve any productive purpose. Sports psychologist, Dr. Richard Coop warns the golfer to avoid the tendency to "connect the dots" or attempt to piece together all the minuscule fragments that constitute the golf swing. For effective play, Dr. Coop suggests going with the feel of a full and fluid swing.

Larry Miller, a former PGA Tour player and author of *Holographic Golf*, suggests that the swing can at very most be broken down into three components—what he refers to as the three static positions. The points of the swing during address, at the top, and in the finish position represent the three static moments in the golf swing, where all motion is temporarily stopped. Miller contends that by studying and committing to practice these three points in the swing, the whole swing will find itself and eventually happen automatically.

The way I manage to continue to develop my fundamentals and at the same time not become too bogged down with mechanics on the course is to employ the use of two practice swings. I take the first one while I'm standing behind my ball and looking at the target. During this practice swing, I concentrate on a fundamental portion of my swing that I am working on, such as a full shoulder turn or keeping my weight inside my right foot at the top. Before hitting, I take a second practice swing that is smooth and rhythmic, giving no thought at all to mechanics. I waste little time before hitting, with the hope that the fluidity of my second practice swing and the mechanics studied during the first one blend together and result in a solid hit.

If you do not feel the need or desire to develop a new swing, you can no doubt improve the quality of your play and increase visits to The Zone with the swing you've used for years. Just remember to make it a point to think in terms of a positive target area, to never use more than one swing thought at a time, and to make every effort to go with a *whole* swing that is rhythmic and not broken down into mechanical components.

Know Your Predominant Sensory Mode

ANOTHER QUALITY THAT IMPROVES YOUR CHANCES OF FINDING The Zone is an understanding of how your senses work. The Zoned-in golfer is making efficient use of sensory input and output. The golfer who is struggling is being bombarded by sensory overload. Sounds, sights, the feel of the club, comfort with stance, a disjointed sense of rhythm join together to confuse and frustrate the golfer who is experiencing poor play. Golfers who have found The Zone are not thinking about these variables. They are on automatic pilot, relying on instinct and feel.

All individuals have a predominant sensory mode that best enables effective learning. This can be observed in children as they first learn to read. Some children learn to read most quickly when they *see* words; others learn most effectively by *hearing* the sounds that make up language. There exists for each of us a sensory mode that most efficiently delivers messages to our brain. Because the golf swing occurs so quickly, information-processing had better be fast and efficient. It is for this reason essential to understand whether your mind responds best to *visual, auditory, or kinesthetic* cues.

Visual Mode. Visual learners have a big advantage when it comes to concentration and the likelihood of Zoned-in play. Such players are said to "have good pictures," or as Jack Nicklaus refers to it, "go to the movies." In his book, *Golf My Way*, Nicklaus says that, "I never hit a shot, even in practice, without having a very sharp, in-focus picture of it in my head. It's like a color movie. First I 'see' the ball where I want it to finish, nice and white and sitting up high on the bright green grass. Then the scene quickly changes and I 'see' the ball going there: its path, trajectory, and shape, even its behavior on landing."

The theory behind visualization is that the subconscious cannot distinguish what it perceives in the mind as opposed to what it sees in the "real world." For any given shot, the subconscious locks into what it has just "seen," and will replicate the visualized shot during the moment when it counts. Why else do you think a great player like Jack Nicklaus would invest so much energy into visualization? And why do you think he has made so many brilliant, if not impossible shots during his career. If you asked him, he would tell you that the great shot you witnessed on television was simply a replay of a shot that had already occurred. A shot that only he was privy to in the movies of his mind.

Visualization is so powerful a technique for effective shotmaking that it would well be worth the effort to develop this skill even if it does not come naturally to you. Begin slowly, by standing behind your ball at the range and picturing the exact flight you would expect an ideally struck ball to take. Continue to watch the ball as it lands, rolls, and finally comes to a stop. You do not even need to be on the range to employ the technique of visualization. The evening before or while on the way to a golf outing, picture yourself on the first tee, hitting a perfect drive down the middle. Deep within your subconscious is a memory bank that stores every such crushed drive, and every shanked pitch shot as well. The more positive memories that are deposited in this bank—be it real or visualized—the more likely it will be that your subconscious will reenact a positive shot when the heat is on.

Auditory Mode. The friend I play golf with most frequently is constantly talking to himself on the golf course. *Putt's goin' to break left to right, aim left edge of the cup . . . . Nice and easy backswing, take it slow, no need to hurry . . . . Take the bunkers out of play, aim for the right side of the green . . .* and so on. An auditory learner like this friend of mine learns best by making use of verbal cues. Auditory golfers typically depend on inner speech to direct their games and, rather than focus on a visual picture of the target, will employ verbal triggers and swing thoughts to get their swings going.

Directing your game through listening or auditory mode can be effective, but brings with it several potentially destructive problems. For one, a necessary requirement for Zoned-in play is a quiet and clear mind. The auditory golfer, with need for verbal cues, is always listening to chatter. It might not be as disruptive as talkative playing partners, but any words passing through conscious awareness create a mental state that is less than ideal.

What do you do if sounds are more easily processed by your brain than visual images? Because your predominant sensory mode is neurologically based, the extent to which you can control the manner in which you process information is limited. If you are an auditory learner, go with it, bearing in mind the problems this learning style can potentially create. For instance, you have to be aware of negative messages that enter your mind during the course of a round. When you are standing on a tee with water to the left, it is easier to visualize a shot landing in the fairway than it is to resist the temptation to tell yourself to "not put the ball in the drink." Such negatively stated verbal messages are the quickest way to get in trouble.

If you must depend on thoughts rather than images, train yourself to think in terms of positive self-statements. In the case of the tee area overlooking water, train your mind to think in terms of the ball landing in the fairway. *Do not* make mention of the water hazard. Use the technique of cognitive restructuring to better ensure that your self-statements are positively oriented. And it wouldn't hurt to incorporate some degree of visualization into the process. Auditory learners are not entirely incapable of seeing images in their "mind's eye." Tell yourself to hit the fairway, and take an extra moment to "see" the successful execution of the shot before you actually attempt it. It will not come easily or naturally for the auditory golfer, but the development of visualization skills is possible and will yield extremely satisfying results.

An interesting auditory technique that promotes the integration of music and movement was presented by Marlin Mackenzie in his book, *Golf: The Mind Game.* Referred to as the M & M Process, Dr. Mackenzie suggests that, instead of verbal cues, the auditory golfer make use of music to facilitate effective performance. The process consists, first, of finding a piece of music that you find pleasing and that also matches your perception of the rhythm of a fluid swing. The next step is to listen to this music, in a relaxed state at home, while imagining a perfect swing. From there you strap on a Walkman at the driving range, the purpose of which is to create a strong association between the selected music and the actual golf swing. Eventually, the music can be listened to in your head or even hummed on the golf course. The association between the selected melody and an effective golf swing should enable smooth and rhythmic timing. The M & M Process just might be a valid approach for some auditory golfers. One look at a calm and cool Fuzzy Zoeller whistling his way around the golf course makes a pretty good case for at least giving this method a try.

Kinesthetic Mode. During a group lesson at a golf school where I was presenting a seminar, a golf professional demonstrated the importance of being aware of the direction of the clubhead at different points in the swing. When he got around to watching my swing, he told me that my clubface was too open at the top of my backswing, making it difficult for me to get it square at impact. This was the reason I tended to push my woods and long irons. He suggested that I increase my awareness of what my clubface was doing at various points during the swing. My first attempt to do so resulted in a whiff. After a few more futile attempts to satisfy his request, I gave up. I simply could not *feel* the position of the clubhead. Any attempt to do so broke down my concentration to the point of complete ineptness.

It's pretty safe to say that I am not what you would call a *feel* player. Stated differently, I do not process information in the kinesthetic mode very effectively. Unfortunately for me, the ability to *feel* a good golf swing is probably the most effective way for finding The Zone. It is also a talent that the greatest golfers in the world have been blessed with. If you rely on kinesthetic cues, such as the feel of a proper shoulder turn, the weight of the golf club in your hands, the sense of motion that you experience as you come through the hitting zone, or the muscular sensations that occur as you set up to the ball, you are in an elite club and should feel very grateful for this ability. Make use of this gift by eliminating all verbal swing thoughts with the possible exception of reminding yourself to employ good rhythm.

Kinesthetic golfers do not have to talk to themselves, thus eliminating the mental clutter that is one of the greatest obstacles to Zoned-in play. If weak in regard to the visual mode for processing information, kinesthetic individuals should still attempt to develop the ability to visualize a shot before it happens. The combination of the feeling and seeing parts of the game creates the optimal sensory scenario for effective golf performance along with regular instances of play in The Zone.

If you are not certain which sensory mode predominates in your golf game and general learning style, experiment with different cues using different sensory modes. Go to the range and commit to hitting twenty consecutive shots relying exclusively on the visual image of the shot you want to hit before actually hitting it. Is it easy or hard for you to create such pictures in your mind? Next, use a verbal swing thought for twenty consecutive shots. Finally try a kinesthetic cue such as the feel of a full turn or the way your body feels when you finish your shot. Be sure that you are not really using a *verbal* description of how your swing *feels*. It must be just a feeling, devoid of any verbal labels. If this does not come naturally for you, or you are not sure what I mean or whether you are doing it right, you are probably not relying on feel alone.

The purpose of this exercise is twofold. First, you want to develop a better understanding of how your brain processes information and experiences sensory input. Second, you want to determine the extent to which you can develop relatively weak sensory modes. You cannot entirely alter the circuitry of your nervous system, but you can at least partially learn to strengthen

weak modes for processing sensory information. If you are pre-
dominately auditory, you will no doubt continue to talk to yourself at the tee and on the putting green. But given the complexity
of the golf swing, along with the difficulty of accessing The Zone,
you would be foolish not to make the effort to broaden your
sensory base as much as is humanly possible.

Defer to Your Subconscious

IT'S THAT MOMENT BETWEEN SLEEPING AND WAKEFULNESS. TWO
obscure women advise my wife and I that they'll be leaving
early. This leaves us with unexpected free time. I decide to run
out to the range to hit balls but will first eat some of the choco-
lates that we had bought for our guests . . . secretly.

What is the hidden meaning of this dream? Could it be that I
need to stuff myself with forbidden culinary delights to fill the
emptiness inside of me that is a result of the shame I feel as a
golfer, an athlete, a man? To be perfectly honest, I don't have a
clue as to the meaning of this dream—or most any dream, for
that matter. But still, I am fascinated by the splendidly creative
extravaganzas that are produced in the studio of my subconscious. I am also convinced that the amazing content of dreams
provides proof of the unlimited mental powers that remain hidden from our conscious awareness. And included in these hidden powers are the secrets about the magic and mystery of The
Zone.

There is a great deal we don't understand about The Zone
and about the workings of our subconscious mind. But we do
recognize that the two are related. When we are playing in The
Zone, our subconscious *knows* that good things are going to happen. We also recognize that self-hypnosis is an effective method
for accessing subconscious levels of thought. It would logically
follow that we can employ self-hypnotic techniques for increasing the likelihood of visiting The Zone.

Offering yourself soothing, positive statements while in a relaxed state imprints these thoughts on subconscious awareness.
You will recall that self-hypnosis was presented as a recommended technique for controlling several of Golf's Mental Hazards. And, of course, overcoming these hazards is an essential

prerequisite for Zoned-in play. But self-hypnosis can also be employed as an advanced method for those who have moved beyond the basics. It can specifically be implemented for the sole objective of increasing the probability of visiting The Zone. And given the elusive ambiguity of the conditions for play in The Zone, what makes more sense than to attempt to instill in your subconscious mind the belief that The Zone is just around the corner, at the next tee.

Make yourself a "Zone tape," a prerecorded message suggesting that you will experience the feelings and attitudes that typically accompany Zoned-in play. The night before an outing, find a comfortable and quiet place where you can practice progressive relaxation and listen to the tape. Make sure you tell yourself that you will be mentally and physically relaxed, calm, alert, and totally focused on each and every shot. Your mind will be clear of all distractions; you will feel energized and will think only of the shot you are facing at the moment. Tell yourself that you will be bursting with confidence, absolutely convinced that you could pull off any shot that is required.

Consider your predominant sensory mode when planning a self-hypnotic Zone tape. The above-stated details would work well for an auditory golfer. If you are a visual golfer, describe the image of yourself enacting a perfect golf swing. If you are familiar with the course you will be playing, describe the view for one or several of the holes, as well as the image of perfect drives that land right where you want them to in the fairway. Play out a few holes completely, and describe the visual detail of each stroke on the way to par or even birdie (this is fantasy . . . go for it!).

If you're a kinesthetic golfer, describe the bodily feelings that you experience when you are on top of your game—the rotation of your trunk, your body turning around your right leg, the feel of the grass under your spikes, the sense of motion when you burst through the hitting zone. Spare no details. You might as well take advantage of your suggestive state and the fact that your subconscious mind is soaking up the details. And remember that when it counts—when the gods are determining who gains entry to The Zone at a particular moment in time—the strong voice lobbying for or against your chances will be that of your subconscious mind.

A Final Note About the Zone

You can overcome Golf's Mental Hazards, develop your concentration skills, strengthen weak areas of sensory processing, practice self-hypnosis religiously, and still only find The Zone on occasion. And this is probably a good thing. Would you really want to go out round after round and shoot exactly even par? Would you want to see the same pros win tournament after tournament? Sounds boring, doesn't it? What makes golf and life so fascinating is the fact that we can never be entirely sure of what to expect or when we might find a little lightning in a bottle.

On the other side of this "bitter with the sweet" philosophy is the necessity of experiencing the flipside of The Zone—that is, the dreaded uglies. Believe it or not, those instances when your game falls apart to a frightening degree—I mean where you actually *cannot* hit a golf ball—must also be experienced from time to time. The Zone and the uglies are actually, in a sense, similar states. They are similar in that they represent bipolar opposites which are necessary end-points on the range of fluctuation. What they share in common is that they both occur with relative infrequency, are inexplicable, do not typify your usual performance, and cannot be controlled.

If you're going through an "ugly" phase in your golf game, it is important to know when it's best to take a break or to simply play through it. If you're absolutely miserable and this state is impacting on your job and personal relations, hang 'em up for a week or two. However, if you can muster up the wisdom and patience to play through the struggling phase, you will benefit in the long run. You have to get through a certain undefined quota of ugly rounds anyway. Your best bet is to lighten up, make the best of a tough time, and take heart in the knowledge that better days can't be too far away.

11

The Whole Golfer

"A sound mind in a sound body, is a short, but full description of a happy state in this world."

—JOHN LOCKE

THE BASIC THEME OF THIS BOOK SUGGESTS THAT YOU CANNOT SEPA-rate the kind of person you are from the manner in which you approach your golf game. This notion ties in with the recent trend of *holism,* or the concept that our minds connect to our bodies which connect to what we eat which connects to the shin bone which connects to our golf game, and so on. Holism refers to the fact that we are one *whole* person who takes each and every part of ourselves into each and every situation. This chapter expands the concept of holism beyond the impact that personality has on golf performance to include the effects that proper diet, exercise, stress management, and interpersonal relationships have on your ability to hit that little white ball with accuracy and conviction.

Proper Diet

THE THING I HATE MOST ABOUT MIDDLE AGE IS THAT, MORE AND more, the things that I love to eat have become bad for me. I can live without Gummi Bears, Caramello bars, and Junior Mints (this one's a tough call), but I'll be darned if I can accept watching my kids eat hot Buffalo wings, loaded potato skins, and battered mozzarella sticks, while I have a piece of skinless broiled chicken, a dry baked potato, and string beans (it does me little good to know that I am allowed *all the salad* that I want). I can, of course, always look forward to my dessert, which consists of a small dish of fresh fruit and a cup of decaf while the kids shove down their hot fudge sundaes.

I don't mean to sound bitter. I certainly understand the importance of watching my cholesterol, blood pressure, and weight. And if I remain absolutely honest with myself, I must admit that I really do experience a far better quality of life when I follow healthy guidelines for proper diet. I have more energy, feel more confident, can free up the "other side" of my closet, and save a bundle on antacids. And perhaps as important as any of the reasons for rightful eating is the fact that I am convinced that my golf game is better when I feed my body a superior brand of fuel.

The extent to which you change your entire approach to diet in order to play better golf is up to you. But since the focus of this book has been to honestly examine nongolf matters that impact on golf performance, nutrition is simply too important an area to omit. Have you ever stopped to think about variations in golf performance as a function of diet? Do you play better or worse after a large breakfast? Does a late dinner the night before an early round influence your level of play? Have you ever varied your caffeine intake before teeing off to determine if it affects your play? If you're like most people, you have probably never given much systematic thought to the relationship between food intake and golf performance.

Collect Data. You spend hundreds if not thousands of dollars on golf. You read instructional books and magazines, talk endlessly with friends on the subject of improvement, take lessons, attend golf schools, and buy new equipment. You will do anything to bring your game up a notch. Yet, you likely ignore the very substantial benefits that proper diet can offer your golf performance.

I didn't pay much attention to diet until a couple of years ago during my annual Myrtle Beach outing. Our hotel is kind enough to include, as part of our golfing package, a breakfast buffet each morning. Not being the type of individual who makes very good decisions at buffets, my breakfast the first morning consisted of two scoops of scrambled eggs, about a dozen strips of bacon, two sausages, one pancake with butter and maple syrup, one piece of French toast, also with butter and maple syrup, two portions of hash brown potatoes with onions, two pieces of buttered rye toast, and to make sure I ate a balanced meal, a bowl of fresh fruit. I washed this all down with about six cups of coffee (caffeinated).

I recall tending the flag on the 15th hole. I glanced around me at the rich green landscape and blue skies, I felt the warm sun and the cool gentle breeze, I marveled at my place in the world at that very moment in time, all the while tasting the bacon which kept repeating on me. I confided my plight to a playing partner—who interestingly chose a breakfast of a half grapefruit and bran muffin with jelly—who responded, "That's why I never eat a big breakfast before I play. It zaps my energy and generally makes me feel like crap." I couldn't help but wonder if the fact that this similarly skilled golfing friend scored twelve strokes better than me was in any way influenced by the food we put in our bodies that morning.

I decided to collect some data on the subject. I began to keep a journal of the food I ate the night before and the morning of golf outings along with my scores on these various occasions. I also included ratings of my energy level and the extent to which I enjoyed myself during the round. Nothing fancy, just a three-point scale represented by good, average, or poor. Although there were instances of poor diet and good play and vice versa, the results indicated that my golf performance as well as the quality of the experience was generally better when I watched my food intake before play. I learned that alcohol and late meals the night before playing disrupted my sleep. Large breakfasts zapped my energy and too much caffeine made me jittery. During the round, I discovered that sugary snacks such as candy bars or donuts provided a quick lift that was very quickly replaced by an energy shortage.

It is not my intention to go into the details of proper nutrition. It is not my area of expertise and there are scores of books in print that explain the advantages of various dietary patterns for enhanced athletic performance. In fact, there now exists a specialized field known as *sports nutrition*, complete with a growing body of research findings, that specifically addresses this area of concern. If you are serious about improving your game, and do not give much thought to the role of proper diet, I would strongly urge you to at least collect your own data on the subject. Keep a journal for a month and observe the correlation between various eating patterns and the level of your play. I think you will be surprised by how substantial an impact food has on your ability to concentrate, your energy level, as well as the enjoyment factor.

Food as an Addiction. If you know that your excess weight or poor eating habits impair your golf game, yet feel unable to improve your dietary pattern, it may be time to consider that you have a substantial problem with food. Eating disorders—including anorexia, bulimia, and compulsive overeating—are perhaps the most pervasive and difficult to change of all psychological problems. Not unlike drugs, alcohol, sex, or gambling, food has the potential to become an addictive disorder. In effect, this means that the substance in question controls you, that you do not control it.

Do you find yourself thinking about food a good deal of the time—what you're going to eat as well as what you are not going to eat? Are you always in the middle of a diet or planning to begin one in the near future? Do you have the tendency to binge late at night, usually when no one is around to observe you? Do you eat in response to emotions such as anxiety, sadness, anger, or even joy? Do you go through periods when you eat very, very little in an attempt to lose weight very quickly? Do not despair if you responded yes to one or several of the above-stated questions. Although it means that you do have some form of eating disorder, it also means that you are like most of the people in the world. Food obsession is far more common than the layperson would ever guess.

How to Deal with a Food Obsession. Like all psychological problems, the first step to helping yourself is to step out of denial and admit that you have a problem. If you are greater than 10 percent above your suggested body weight, if you are a chronic dieter, if you are always thinking about food, you would benefit by dealing with the problem. Bear in mind that there are worse things than being overweight or having poor dietary habits. Surely, you are no menace to society. No one has ever been ticketed for *driving while bloated*, and food is not mood-altering to the extent of some more volatile addictive substances such as drugs or alcohol. This is part of the reason that food is probably the most difficult addiction to get a handle on. Not only does society not discourage overeaters, we encourage them. If anything, your host or hostess is offended if you *do not* overeat. And also, food is one substance that cannot be entirely abstained from. Unlike cigarettes or alcohol, we must eat to live. It is far more difficult to make decisions regarding quantity of intake than it is to simply give something up altogether.

If you want to improve your health, longevity outlook, appearance, self-confidence, and golf swing, proper diet and weight are important parts of these matters. If you cannot get it together with food, consider getting some professional help. Talk to your physician and consider working with a nutritionist or some other structured weight-control program. Problems with food are best served when you are monitored and especially when you are aided by a support group. My personal favorite place to refer "food addicts" is to *Overeaters Anonymous*. This is a worldwide organization that is based on the principles of the same Twelve Step program that has successfully helped alcoholics and drug addicts through the years. I would advise you to read some literature about this program and, if you are really motivated, to delve into the complicated dynamics that make up the psychology of food problems, take the plunge, and attend a meeting.

The Importance of Exercise

AMERICA'S BASEMENTS ARE FILLED WITH UNUSED STATIONARY bikes, treadmills, and rowing machines; a testimony to the difficulty of sticking with an exercise program. It seems that despite the clear-cut evidence linking physical exercise to enhanced quality of life and longevity, the average individual has difficulty finding the time for this critical activity. Most people continue to delude themselves with the belief that they are immortal, that "it can't happen to me." This notion is supported by the fact that oftentimes the most conscientious followers of a regular exercise program are people who have had some kind of a scare—perhaps a heart attack or the threat of one. For these "enlightened" individuals, their bodies have become as vulnerable, fragile, and unpredictable as their putting strokes.

The nature of my work has me peering through a clear window into reality everyday. It is a reality where bad things can happen to good people, where young people can have their bodies fail them, where the unexpected and unfair *can* occur. I realize that it is not healthy to dwell on the unlikely tragedies that can befall any one of us at any given moment, and it is not my intent to encourage you to begin reading the obituaries every morning. But it is equally important to not go in the other direction and ignore the truth about the clear-cut benefits of regular exercise.

If you want to be one of those people who point out that a young world-class athlete can suddenly and inexplicably drop dead, or that your grandfather smoked three packs of Camels and ate eggs cooked in bacon fat for every day of his ninety-two years, go ahead and kid yourself. We all know that these are the exceptions and not the rule and that there are no guarantees. But the simple truth is that a better conditioned individual is in a better position to live a long and natural life than someone who is out of shape. Add to the longevity factor, the additional "quality-of-life" bonuses which include enhanced self-confidence, regular post-workout "highs" that result from the release of endorphins into your bloodstream, better management of the stress in your life, and yes of course . . . an improved golf game.

Many people do not regard golf as a *real* sport since it can be played by most anyone, regardless of physical condition. This might be true to a certain extent; however, the complete truth is that, all things being equal, good physical conditioning will definitely result in a higher caliber of play. The following are some of the ways that golf performance can be improved by aerobic and flexibility conditioning.

Finishing Strong. When I have a league match during the summer months, I hope for hot and humid weather. I find dry and moderate conditions to be more pleasant, but feel I have an advantage when the weather is more on the extreme side. For the meager two hours I invest each week in an aerobic exercise routine, I feel confident in the security that I am at very least as well conditioned as my opponent and that I will not lose simply because of the oppressive weather conditions. The way I figure it, there are already enough reasons for potentially poor play that I cannot control. I *can*, however, control my decision to condition myself to the point of feeling secure in the belief that I will not get worn down or fatigued during the critical, latter holes of a match.

Avoiding Injuries. Watch the pros play the game, and the unknowing observer will undoubtedly conclude that golf is an effortless game that leaves opponents looking as clean, dry, and unruffled after a match as they appeared on the first tee. Your average recreational golfer knows better. Follow a foursome of hackers around for 18 holes and you'll see a whole different sight. Sweaty, disheveled, exhausted, and mumbling, these golfers know they have been part of an intensely fought battle with the course, the elements, and their playing partners, not to mention their bodies and minds.

The average golfer's swing does not appear as effortless as that of a professional golfer. Add to the strain of swinging from the heels, ripping over the top, hitting them fat, thin, from every which angle, the fact that the weekend golfer takes a lot *more* swings than the professional. Hips rotating, shoulders turning, arms flying across a hopefully steady head, and you have the potential for all kinds of bodily harm. A slight strain between the shoulder blades, a sore left pinkie, a strained wrist, an achy arch, a stiff neck, and lower back pain are just a few of the multitude of nagging injuries that could effectively throw off the golfer's timing just enough to make square contact about as unlikely as a bogey-free round.

Preround stretching and a series of practice swings of gradually increasing forcefulness are an absolute must for avoiding injury on the golf course. Beyond this minimum requirement is the suggestion that you commit yourself to a regular program of flexibility exercises. I use a set of weighted machines known as *Cybex* three times a week after my aerobic workout. I keep the weights light and do as many as twenty to thirty repetitions. My motive for this program is far more practical than vain. I have, after all, no delusions of a chiseled physique at this stage of my life. It is flexibility that I am seeking to accomplish. I believe in the benefit of this routine as supported by the fact that I have not had any muscle pulls or strains for several years. Even with my history of lower back problems some ten years ago, I rarely experience any back pain at this stage in the life of my aging body. And even though my exercise program has not substantially improved my somewhat negative body image, I still take pride in the knowledge that beneath my outer shell of flab, I am tight as a drum!

Confidence. Henry Ford was quoted as saying, "If you think you can or you think you can't, you're always right." In the decades that have passed since this statement was first issued, volumes have been written about theories and methods for self improvement as well as for golf improvement. Despite all the scholarly hoopla, Mr. Ford's simple and truthful statement about the importance of confidence maintains its stronghold at the top of the list of requisites for the pursuit of success.

Few things in this life will make you feel better and more confident about yourself than being in good physical condition. It logically follows that this feeling of augmented self-confidence will generalize to your golf game. How can it not? If you look better, feel stronger and more energized, how can you not have a little more zest in your swing? And you'll find that even if you don't play as well as you had hoped to, the general good feeling that comes from improved physical conditioning will, to a great extent, compensate for the disappointment of substandard play. I know that after a particularly bad outing, I can't wait to get to the club and have a good workout. It burns off the negative feelings, lifting my spirits and energy level. What I most enjoy is that there is no scoring, no judgments about quality of performance for an aerobic workout. Just put your time in and rate the outcome par for the course.

To Steady Nerves. If you are a Hazard One golfer, physical exercise is an absolute must. You will recall that the overactivity of your autonomic nervous system can potentially result in muscle tension and an impaired ability to concentrate. Physical exercise is a healthy and productive way to burn off the excess adrenaline in the gym instead of at the first tee. Even if Hazard One is not one of your elevated mental hazards, you still experience problems with nerves at the first tee or during critical moments of a match. Everyone does. The anti-anxiety benefits of physical exercise are too substantial for any golfer to regard as unnecessary for game improvement.

In addition to general conditioning, there are specific exercises that have been developed for the purpose of enhancing golf performance. I refer the interested reader to either Gary Player's book *Fit for Golf* or the PGA-endorsed *Exercise Guide to Better Golf*, by Dr. Frank Jobe, et. al.

Stress Management

THERE IS A SCENE IN WOODY ALLEN'S CLASSIC MOVIE *ANNIE HALL* where he depicts life as being divided into two categories of people—the horrible and the miserable. Allen's character in the movie details the theory: "The horrible would be like terminal cases, you know, like blind and crippled. I don't know how they get through life. It's amazing to me. And the miserable . . . that's everyone else. So when you go through life, you should be thankful that you're miserable."

However bleak Mr. Allen's perspective on the state of life may appear, it remains true that everyone is necessarily to some extent "miserable." Stated differently, it is impossible to live a life devoid of stress and the unpleasantness that accompanies it. Health problems, financial difficulty, marital problems, difficulty with children, all qualify as substantial sources of stress. Although not everyone experiences all areas of stress to the same degree, it is a certainty that everyone will have to deal with at least some of the above-stated examples of stress at some point in life. What determines quality of life is the extent to which you manage stressful circumstances and thus keep the inevitable misery at an absolute minimum.

The Stress Will Come with You. The whole person comes to the golf course with accumulated stress weighing heavily on performance. Have you ever run from the office to the first tee without a chance to take a breath and get prepared for the physical and mental challenge of actually playing the game? Chances are that your backswing was as quick and choppy as the manner in which you drove to the golf course. Stop and consider what you are doing. Golf is your primary source of recreation, your opportunity to escape from the stressful demands of your everyday life. By squeezing your golf game into an overcrowded schedule, you are missing out on the wonderful stress-management potential that the game can potentially provide. In fact, add a highly probable crummy performance to the mix, and if anything, you've succeeded in escalating the stress level in your life.

I recall reading somewhere that the Japanese surround their golf outings with a ritual that includes extravagant meals, the use of caddies, and a postround sauna. I recognize that the average Western "working stiff' does not have the time or affluence to afford themselves such indulgence, but there are compromise positions that can be considered. If, for example, your weekday tee-time is 5:00 P.M., how about getting to the course at 4:00? I recognize that this might not be easy to arrange, but if you absolutely *had* to be out of your office by 3 :30, you would somehow manage to do it. Make it a top priority. That's the only way you will do it. I believe that it *should* be a top priority and recommend it for your physical and mental health.

Drive to the course at a slow, leisurely pace, listening to soothing music or perhaps to a self-hypnotic tape. When you arrive, slowly and methodically put your shoes on, put your tees and balls, watch and wallet in their assigned places, and take a leisurely stroll to the practice range. When you get there, take some time to stretch and loosen up, and then hit a handful of balls. If you like the way they're flying, don't hit more than a dozen or so; use the extra time on the putting green. If your timing is off, hit a few more. If you can't get it going, make sure to give yourself time to practice your putting anyway. You know from previous experience that putting will affect your score more than any other part of your game. And you also know that there is not necessarily a strong correlation between how you hit them at the range and how it goes when the bell rings.

Get to the first tee at least fifteen minutes before you tee off. Already warmed up, you might as well take the opportunity to socialize with your playing partners for the day. No need to stand off to the side, loading your brain with mechanical details and continuing to practice your swing. Let it go at this point. Your game will be more benefited by relaxed mingling than it will by intensive attention to swing detail. All you can do is to give each and every stroke your full attention, and wait and see what the results will be. Running to the tee, saying your hellos and how-are-yous while huffing up the first fairway in a distracted state, is the best way to get off poorly, and in effect write off the round before it even begins.

Why Stress Is Not All Bad. When Olympic speed-skater Dan Jansen rallied from personal tragedy and the disappointment over his performance in the 1988 Games to come back and win the 1,000 meters in 1994, it was a glowing statement about the potential positive power of stress. Dr. James E. Loehr, the sports psychologist who worked with Dan and the author of *The New Toughness Training for Sports,* believes that people should actually attempt to seek out forms of mental and physical stress, citing it as "the stimulus for growth." During an interview with *USA Weekend,* he went on to say that "without stress the process of weakening begins. If we're going to get tougher, we have to be stress seekers."

Dr. Loehr is not suggesting that you quit your job, pick a fight with your spouse, and put a bid on a house you can't afford. Rather he is suggesting that in addition to the negative instances of stress that befall us and that we cannot entirely control, there are positive forms of stress that we can elect to experience. In the physical realm, it can be some form of exercise. On the mental side, it can be learning a new activity such as bridge or chess, or selecting new and challenging reading material. The basic premise behind the notion of positive stress is that it be represented by an activity that is somewhat novel and moderately challenging.

Central to Dr. Loehr's theory is the recovery from stress. He expands his comment about stress seeking with the idea that

"The other side to that, which is equally important, is that stress unabated by recovery can kill you. So you have to balance stress with recovery." He describes sleep as the most important path to recovery from physical stress. As for mental stress, Dr. Loehr suggests talking out your feelings with good friends, possibly with a therapist, or even writing down your feelings in a journal. A final suggestion is to find the opportunity to laugh. Humor is a proven method for stress reduction that you would be well advised to seek out. When going through one of those "stressed to the max" phases, watch a silly movie or call a friend who makes you laugh. Do it because you'll feel better and also because your body needs the calm, restful effect of a good, hearty laugh.

Remember to Be Grateful. When life is going well, you will be in a position to seek out the kind of stress that it positive and will result in positive growth. No one wants the kind of stress that comes with phone calls in the middle of the night or an unexpected and inexplicable bodily pain. But don't lull yourself into believing that a calm and relaxed life is represented by zero stress. This way of thinking runs counter to human nature. If your health is sound, you *will* worry about money, the kids, or your golf game. If all is going well, something will pop up— perhaps the car will make a strange noise or the microwave will break. Just don't get caught up in the minutiae of ridiculous distracting sources of stress. If your life is running smoothly, don't sit back and wait for something to go wrong. Find a new challenge or pursuit that will stretch you to new limits. And remember to be grateful for the good fortune of living a life that is, at very worst, nothing more than miserable.

Interpersonal Relationships

To varying degrees, we are all social creatures who require relationships with other people to feel complete. Not everyone needs the excitement of large, crowded, and noisy parties—in fact, many would shy away from such events—but all people require the opportunity to, every now and then, converse with someone they feel comfortable with, a person they can trust.

Relationships are difficult. And ironically, the closer and more intimate they become, the more difficult they are to sustain peacefully. Marriage is the best example. How many married couples do you know who get along smoothly, who both feel that they are appreciated in the relationship, who aren't entangled in some sort of power struggle, who do not bicker? Another example is parents and children. A kid can behave perfectly in school, yet be entirely obstinate and oppositional when left to deal one-on-one with mom or dad. We are not comfortable enough with casual acquaintances to reveal our complete and honest selves. So instead we wear "social masks," and save our most obnoxious behavior for the people who really love us.

The state of the relationships in your life is a part of the whole you that you take to work, bring home at night, and yes . . . take to the golf course. I recall an instance where I had an argument with my wife the night before an important golf outing. I was playing with an out-of-town friend whom I rarely got to see, and very much wanted the experience to be pleasant. Translated into the language of the golfer, I really needed to play well.

Maybe it was the pressure of the workweek, maybe I was uptight because the weather forecast called for showers the next day. I cannot say for sure. What I can state with complete accuracy is that the fight was plain and simply my fault. I can admit this now, but back when it occurred I did not believe this to be the case. It seems that I came home from work in one of my "headhunting" moods, determined to unleash some pent-up frustration through a good fight. When I walked in the door, I began by asking questions I already knew the answer to. For instance, I asked, "Did you check the mail?" knowing full well that my wife has this occasional tendency to sometimes forget to do so. I know it's childish and petty, but sometimes you just can't help but look for trouble.

I won't give the other details (such as my reaction to my wife's annoying manner of eating potato chips or that my socks were in the laundry basket downstairs and not in my dresser drawer where they obviously belonged). Suffice it to say that the argument escalated beyond petty details and we soon managed to find fault with the essence of each other's basic character. In effect, we had the same impossible-to-resolve fight we have had approximately four times a year throughout the twenty-two years of our marriage.

We went to bed that night in a state of cool silence. The following morning, I thought that I had put the disagreement out of my mind when I arrived at the course at 6:15. My friend and I were teamed with a husband and wife, Allen and Pam, and as much as I tried to convince myself otherwise, I couldn't get around the fact that I was feeling grumpy, tired, and highly distracted. My mind refused to stop debating with my wife. I have a tendency to engage in this practice of solitary dialogue. It guarantees that I get to make my point as I see it, without interference or resistance. The problem was the manner in which my highly agitated and distractible state interfered with my ability to find any kind of rhythm and, for that matter, experience any emotion remotely related to enjoyment throughout the course of the 18 holes we played that day.

What also didn't help was the play of Pam—and her husband's unbelievable patience with his wife's horrible level of play. It all began when she teed up a pink ball on one. Typically, I am very tolerant about such matters, and honestly don't mind playing with women. But Pam was so awful, and I was in such a miserable mood, and Allen kept saying, over and over again, "Nice shot, hon," "Good swing, you just peeked a little," "That's the way to follow through." All the while, Pam was hitting dribblers, her best shot of the day traveling maybe fifty yards (she outdrove me on this hole).

After the round, I went to buy a soda in the clubhouse and ran into Allen.

"The weather really cooperated," he said. "I didn't think that low pressure system could miss us."

"I kind of wish it did rain," I answered. "Would have been spared the misery."

"You didn't play so bad. Hit some nice-looking shots."

"You *are* positive," I replied.

"Gotta be positive with this game," he went on. "You'll lose your mind if you're not."

I stepped up to pay the cashier while Allen picked up a couple of burgers. I turned around and saw Pam at their table. She waved and I smiled back. I just had to ask Allen.

"I have to give you credit," I addressed him while I paid the cashier.

He paused while he counted his change and then looked up at me. "What do you mean?"

"Your patience with Pam. I definitely don't have your temperament."

"Temperament's got nothing to do with it. You think it's always been this way? Hell no. Married for thirty-three years. After a while some things sink into the thickest of skulls. She's a good lady who puts up with all of my nonsense. Why get down on her and get myself all bent out of shape in the process? You know, it all goes together."

It all goes together. Allen's words, not mine. I'm the psychologist, the so-called expert, and every once in a while, I get rocked out of my all-knowing trance of self-delusion and learn a lesson from the most unlikely of sources. I went home that night and made my amends with my wife. A simple "I'm sorry" and I knew we would be fine until the next replay a few months down the road.

I don't know if I would have played any better that day if I had avoided the prior night's argument or if I had apologized before going to sleep. But I do know that the whole golfer brings every part of him to the golf course, and a big piece of anybody is the state of his personal relationships—whether with a spouse, a co-worker, friend, significant other, or child. Remember that it's not easy to line up a sharp-breaking, six-foot, downhill putt when you're replaying an unsettling argument that occurred earlier in the day. To play better golf, keep your house in order. Significant interpersonal relationships need to be given time and attention. If an inevitable argument remains unresolved, make amends before running off to play. You'll feel good about yourself, and your mind will be cleared for the task at hand.

12

The Old and the New

"It is a good idea to obey all the rules
when you're young just so you'll have the
strength to break them when you're old."

—MARK TWAIN

BEGINNINGS AND ENDINGS ARE THE MOST CRITICAL AS WELL AS difficult portions of any sequential process. Run a marathon and at the start you need to loosen up, adapt to weather conditions, and assess your energy level before you hit a stride and "cruise" through the middle portion of the race. Get to the last few miles, and again there is the need to evaluate your physical status, to make crucial decisions that pertain to strategy, to dig down deep and determine if there are any reserves that can be drawn upon. A boxer also recognizes the significance of beginnings and endings. He wants to begin a round strongly and finish it with a flurry if he's going to get the judge's attention and a favorable scoring decision. And remember the key to getting a good grade on a paper in high school or college? Make sure the introduction and conclusion are strong and don't worry too much about the middle portions. Everyone knows that teachers are reading and forming judgments most carefully when they first begin and when they finally conclude reading your paper.

Life follows the same principle. The early years are critical for the development of motor skills, social and moral judgment, cognition, and self-esteem. In early adulthood, the reasonably

well-adjusted individual hits a stride based on a sense of competence—of no longer being a child. The young adult often devel-
ops feelings of omnipotence and immortality along with the
belief that anything in life is possible. Somewhere along the way,
however, we wake up. Perhaps it is based in the gradual decline
of physical prowess, in seeing our own children grow up, or
watching our parents grow old. Whatever the reason, there
comes a day when we recognize clearly and without question
that our days on this planet are numbered. If we are going to
enjoy the rest of the time allotted to us, we had better adjust our
ways of thinking and acting.

Once we recover from the shock of mortality, there comes a
"moment of truth"—some might call it a midlife crisis—that is
critical to adjustment during our senior years. Some individuals
do not fare particularly well at this point; they become rigid,
restricted, afraid to venture outside of the confines of comfortable, tried and true experience. Others act out with impulsive
wholesale lifestyle changes in a desperate attempt to convince
themselves that they still have it. Others who successfully pass
through this phase find that life can indeed begin at 40, or 50, or
for that matter 75 or 90. These enlightened individuals have
given up the impossible battle against the insurmountable opponent of time, and have mustered up the courage to live a full and
authentic life—a life that is better than in previous years because
of experience and the wisdom that comes with it.

The game of golf reflects the life process and therefore follows
the principles that apply to beginnings and endings. There are
special conditions that apply to junior and senior golfers—each
with their own unique set of problems and advantages. The
young golfer does not have to overcome years of bad habits and
remains malleable and receptive to new forms of learning. This
same young individual—who gets easily frustrated and bored
—has to struggle to stay on task and maintain a span of attention
throughout the downtime that is so much a part of a round of
golf.

The senior golfer has lost muscle tone and very likely has to
play through an assortment of aches and pains. Motor memory
is so entrenched that even the most subtle of swing changes is
extremely difficult to learn. On the other hand, the mature golfer

has the benefit of patience and self-acceptance which make the inevitable frustrations of the game far easier to deal with than during younger days. Senior adults also have a better perspective on their lives and are more likely to breathe the fresh air and appreciate the gift of walking a golf course with people whose company they enjoy.

The following sections in this chapter will address the psychological advantages of being a junior or senior golfer. There is no need to focus on the problems that these age groups face. If you have ever brought a youngster to a golf course or are beyond your peak physical years, you are well aware of these trouble spots. Golf is a game that is best served by an emphasis on the positive, with an attitude that sees problems as nothing more than obstacles to be solved and overcome.

The Psychological Advantage for Juniors

HOW MANY TIMES HAVE YOU HEARD A GOLFER MAKE THE STATE-ment, "If I had only begun the game when I was young." As a golfer who first picked up a 7-iron at the age of 40, I share this sentiment. It is so difficult to teach my body to perform in new and different ways. Even the adults I know who only became serious about their games when they were too old for more strenuous activities are at an advantage if they played even a little golf during their formative years. However imperfect, their swings reflect a fluidity, purpose, and comfort, as if hitting a golf ball is an activity that is a part of who they are.

Kids Are Sponges. Children are in the midst of the rapidly changing process of development. Their bodies, minds, and neurological systems are in an ongoing state of flux and are thereby highly receptive to new forms of experience and learning. Consider, for example, the foreigner who comes to this country at the age of 6. Already well versed in a native tongue, this child will learn English with little effort and speak it as an adult without any noticeable accent.

I took piano lessons beginning at the age of 6. Although I hardly ever play anymore, I still can play from memory many of the songs I learned as a child. When I tackle a new piece of music, I can keep my gaze on the sheet music while my hands move octaves up and down the keyboard and accurately find the proper keys. Although I find it amazing to be able to do this, it can be simply explained as a matter of well-entrenched motor memory that was developed during the early, critical years of my development. For a middle-aged man, the process of programming a fundamentally correct golf swing into motor memory is a far more difficult matter.

Parents who want to do right by their child should expose them to a wide range of diverse activities. Kids are sponges who soak up everything that passes before their senses. Early experiences, such as language, music, and sports, become *imprinted* upon their developing neurological systems. When a behavior becomes imprinted, it means that it becomes a part of the brain's basic structure. For adults, it is too late for imprinting to occur. Their brains and patterns of neurological functioning are already deeply entrenched. Beyond childhood, learning a foreign language, to play a musical instrument, to ski fearlessly down a mountain, to execute a fundamentally correct golf swing is not unlike electrically rewiring a house after construction is complete. Parts of the existing structure must be torn apart and reassembled. Matters have to get substantially more messy before any progress can be observed.

Bear in mind that exposing young children to various activities is not the same as forcing activities upon them or bombarding them with a constant barrage of athletic and cultural pursuits. Most children will begin activities with an intense level of interest which will quickly fade. Don't belittle them for this loss of interest. Don't call them quitters. Just continue to provide opportunities for new and different activities. It doesn't matter what the activity is. Your objective is to have them maintain an enthusiasm for any type of learning.

How to Introduce Your Child to Golf. Most kids are not that interested in golf. Baseball, football, basketball, and hockey better satisfy their needs for faster pace and team involvement. If you want to gauge your child's interest for golf or just expose a child to the sport, invite him or her to join you at the range. Provide a single, cut-down, highly lofted club, and then turn away. Don't instruct, don't become annoyed if interest wanes, and most important, don't be critical.

If there is some degree of interest demonstrated, sign the child up for a lesson with a professional who has a reputation for working well with children. The social component of a small group lesson might make the experience more enjoyable. Ask the pro's advice on your child's physical and mental readiness for moving things along. If skill and interest levels continue to grow, go out on the par-three courses and keep matters light. Hit a few tee shots, tee a couple up in the fairway, try a little chipping and putting. I strongly recommend that you don't keep score until your kid is adept enough to advance the ball with some degree of consistency. The structure of properly routinized golf is important to learn, but only when the time is right. You have to figure that your kid will probably not have the early intensity of a Phil Mickelson or Tiger Woods. Your only objective during the early stages should be to make the game fun, so that when the time comes—perhaps in twenty or thirty years—there will be pleasant associative memories of time spent on a golf course with mom or dad.

Create a Sense of Success. The LPGA's Teaching and Club Professional Division has recently initiated a program for inner-city kids in the Los Angeles area. With lives surrounded by poverty, violence, and neglect, these children are provided with an opportunity to work toward goals and experience the joy of success through the game of golf. The program's executive director, Andree Martin, says, "Golf helps children develop strong skills of discipline and respect. It also helps develop self-esteem and motivation. The children will need those skills on the golf course and in their personal lives."

In his *Little Red Book,* Harvey Penick suggests that all children should experience the joy of feeling successful in the early stages of their involvement with the game. To accomplish this feeling, he suggests that children learn golf "starting at the cup and progressing back toward the tee." It is his opinion that "The best stroke in the world is not much good without touch or feel. An individual looking stroke that the child has confidence in and a feel for how to use, and that puts the ball close to the hole, is the best stroke in the world for that child." I agree with Mr. Penick's psychological wisdom in this matter. It is very much in accord with the notion of providing the child with an experience that is enjoyable and memorable. Even the child who is a raw beginner will derive the greatest benefit from an experience that results in some degree of success.

The Importance of Role-Modeling. During the fifteen years I have worked with children and their parents, I have repeatedly observed parents display the very behavior that they cannot tolerate in their child. The parental expectation of "do as I say, not as I do" quite simply does not work. Although kids have a mind of their own, and oftentimes a personality that is very different from one or both of their parents, they will invariably pick up mannerisms and attitudes that they have observed in the home.

During the past year, my 9-year-old son has demonstrated a good deal of interest in golf. He has progressed rapidly and we enjoy playing the executive courses together. Out of curiosity, I recently administered to him a modified version of the *MHAS*. His most substantially elevated score was for Hazard Three. "I'm not surprised," I said as I informed him of the results. "Remember last month, when you hit that green, were thinking birdie, and four-putted for a double?" I reminded him of how down he became, to the point where his game fell apart for the next several holes. I also reminded him of his comments about giving up the game and sticking to baseball.

A short lecture later, my son reminded me of my own reaction to an ugly round that occurred only a few short days before his four-putt experience. He recalled my comment that I stunk and was going to stick with the par-three courses because that's where I belonged.

No one needs his kid mouthing off at him like that, particularly when the kid is making a valid point. The truth is that I am a Hazard Three golfer who continues to occasionally experience that sick, sinking feeling in response to poor play. "That's right, son," I replied. "I *do* get too down on myself once in awhile. But I've made a lot of progress. I don't nearly get as down on myself as I used to." He gave me that "whatever you say, dad" look, which meant that he knew the deal and wasn't about to expend any more energy attempting to convert me to his more rational way of thinking.

You know your weaknesses as a golfer and as a person. If you want to see your kid develop a well-adjusted, if not classy demeanor on or off the golf course, get your own act together. If you slam your club into the turf in Hazard Two fashion, figure your child will do the same when faced with frustrating circumstances. If you kick your ball, cheat on your score, or give yourself putts that are inside of three feet, expect the young golfers in your family to pick up the same habits. Simply stated, be the kind of person you want your child to be. If you can't pull it off, don't be surprised to observe faults in the character of the children who look for you to show them the way.

The Psychological Advantage for Seniors

DURING MY EARLY GOLFING DAYS, I MADE A HABIT OF GOING OFF as a single to various courses on weekday mornings. Part of my reason was based on the flexibility in my work schedule and the uncrowded conditions during the working week. Another reason was that I would typically be hooked up with seniors. And as a struggling, highly inconsistent beginner, there were no better playing partners than old, seasoned golfers. They say that oversized woods and cavity-back irons are the most forgiving parts of the golf game. I disagree. Seniors get my vote. Hit a tee shot OB or chip one over the green, and you can count on an old-timer to ease the pain by telling you that your game's got promise and that with a little practice and patience, you'll be coming around before you know it.

Not all senior adults have developed the kind of tolerant and patient attitude that I have just described. There are those who are bitter, who resent the lack of appreciation that today's younger people have for the way things used to be. Of course, their perspective of days gone by is a glorified reconstruction. They recall a time when people had respect for one another, were less wasteful, appreciated the value of hard work and of a dollar. It is not my place to present a sociocultural discussion of people from generations past, but I can state with some degree of certainty that the seniors who dwell on the "olden days," who believe that the youth in their day were a cut above the young people of today, who continue to repeat the same old "war stories" to anyone who will listen, have not adjusted well to the changes and loss that are a necessary part of the process of growing older.

The remaining sections of this chapter will focus on the perspective and attitudes of those seniors who are playing life's "back nine" with dignity and class. On and off the golf course, the positive outlook, good cheer, and open-mindedness of these remarkable individuals are a source of inspiration to us all. They provide us with the hope that we too can make life's "turn" with some style, self-respect, and a whole lot of fun.

Tomorrow's Life Is Too Late. They say that youth is wasted on the young, and I guess to some extent this statement is true. If we could feel the strength and energy of youth and couple it with the wisdom that experience has ingrained in us, it would no doubt be a fantastic life. The only problem is that this cannot happen outside of the fantasy of science-fiction or wishful thinking. Youth *is* perhaps wasted on the young, *must be* wasted on the young, but the real tragedy occurs when old age is wasted on the old. Rather than take advantage of the benefits of life experience and wisdom, we look back and dream of what could have been, still ignoring—as we did while busy wasting our youth—the very real fact that there is a today that needs to be lived.

I recall playing with Mort, an 85-year-old man who left a very powerful impression on me. My friend and I were paired with Mort and his young 75-year-old sidekick named Sam. On the first hole, I watched Mort set up to his tee shot. A tall, thin, regal-looking man, it was obvious that he had been around the game for a long time. Intensely focused, going through a routine that must have been repeated thousands upon thousands of times, Mort took a weak, constricted but rhythmic swing that flushly spanked the ball and sent it straight down the fairway, about 150 yards out. Mort struggled to bend down and retrieve his tee and had to grasp at it several times before successfully grabbing it, examining it, and placing it in his pocket. This process alone appeared to be exhausting.

Mort's straight-ahead, trouble-free, steady play, and good short game resulted in a 48 for nine holes. Throughout the round, Mort's only comments pertained to a good play one of us made, the beautiful weather, and how great it was to be out on a golf course. He took note of flowers by the tee areas, expressed dismay at the sight of a beautiful weeping willow that had been damaged by lightning, and expressed no dissatisfaction with the slow, struggling foursome ahead of us.

I was into my usual frantic mode of trying to play good golf, a mind-set that results in very little recollection of the details of the round, let alone an appreciation for the beauty that surrounds me. I was also less tolerant of the foursome ahead and paced around the tee area of the par-three 8th watching the players scan the woods for what appeared to be at least two very lost balls. Observing my agitated state, Mort suggested that I relax and take a seat on the bench alongside of him.

As I sat down, Mort turned and made direct eye contact with me. "What do you do for a living?"

"I'm a psychologist," I replied.

"That figures," said a smiling Mort.

"Why do you say that?" I asked.

"You're a nervous young man," he responded. "I hear that all you fellas are a little bit whacko."

I couldn't help but laugh. "You're right. Except I'm much better adjusted than the average shrink."

I looked up at Sam who had placed his ball on the tee and then back at Mort. At first glance I categorized them both as seniors, but on closer examination, there was obviously a world of difference. Sam still gave the appearance of strength. Mort, on the other hand, seemed frail and had a choppy motion about him. Studying Mort's profile, I could see the concentration of lines. Hundreds of multidirectional lines. Like his movements, his physical presence had also been reduced to fragments. I wondered if this is what happens when we get older, if we lose our uniform oneness—as if we are, in fact, coming apart at the seams.

Climbing the hill at 9, I continued to study Mort. I was tired and a little bit cranky, and there was Mort, slowly putting one foot in front of the other, his head turning back and forth, his senses soaking up the world that surrounded him. The more I marveled at Mort's courage and class, the more ashamed I felt about myself. I bounce up the fairway, don't think twice about bending over to tee up a ball, take a strong and pain-free rip at the ball, and moan if a shot is not close to perfect. I looked at Mort and felt ashamed at how much of my life I take for granted —at how many moments and days slip by unnoticed because I am too distracted by the pettiness of my self-absorption and the sound of my whining. I felt the need to "wake up" and lock-in the realization that, if fortunate enough, it would be my turn someday.

My experience with Mort to this point was already memorable and offered some important lessons about how to live. But it was what he told me upon shaking hands and saying our good-byes that has stuck with me. Mort had terminal cancer and was scheduled for major surgery four days from the day that he noticed the flowers and mourned for the damaged willow. He told me that he wouldn't be playing any more golf that season, and in all likelihood, had just completed his final round.

Driving away from the course, and for the next several days, I wondered if Mort was so tuned in to his surroundings, so much alive in the moment, because he knew that it might have been his final round. I concluded that this was probably not the case. I figured that a man like Mort spent a good deal of his life taking the time to look around and savor the joyful and amazing moments that life occasionally affords to those who are wise enough to watch for them. I don't think that an individual who was not blessed with the courage and serenity that Mort displayed would have been out playing golf at all under such dreadful circumstances. It takes a special kind of person, who has worked long and hard on his life, to play each and every round of golf as if it might be the last one he ever plays.

Necessary Adjustments. There is a saying that "If life gives you lemons, make lemonade." I guess this would translate to the senior golfer as "If life gives you arthritis, buy oversized, graphite-shafted clubs." Along with advancing age come the very real problems of declining muscle tone, decreasing strength, and lesser agility. These are problems that make the game of golf more difficult. If not compensated for, they result in a poorer quality of play. Of course, the physical decline that accompanies advancing age creates problems, not just on the golf course, but in all aspects of life. In response to the challenge of aging, the senior faces one of three choices: (1) to be depressed, (2) to be gracefully accepting, or (3) to invest in lemons and high-tech golf equipment.

Jack Nicklaus has had a whole lot to say during his first few years of eligibility for the Senior Tour. In response to the need to compensate for some decline in what was once a tremendously powerful swing, Nicklaus has made several adjustments that have helped him maintain his competitive edge. Whereas his solid distance once allowed him to hit about 75 percent of greens in regulation, he now hits them maybe 60 percent of the time. To compensate for this drop-off, Nicklaus has worked harder than ever on his short game and putting.

Nicklaus has also changed the selection of clubs he carries in his bag. He explains, "I never would have believed even twenty years ago that there would come a time when I would leave out a long iron in favor of a fairway wood, but I've done that with a 5- or a 7-wood a number of times since becoming a senior." In addition to hard work and equipment changes, Nicklaus has also modified lifestyle habits such as the incorporation of a more sensible dietary plan and increased exercise in his daily routine. This great champion is not wasting his energy bemoaning the loss of his once magnificent skills. Still possessed by the will of a champion, Nicklaus will do everything that is humanly possible to adjust his game and along the way no doubt snatch another handful of victories.

If you're thinking that you are no Jack Nicklaus, that you couldn't hit a golf ball at age 21 as well as Jack will probably manage when he's 75, you have missed the point. Take a moment to read between the lines and learn something that goes well beyond the scope of ball striking from this great man. Do you think for a minute that Jack Nicklaus likes it when the drives of younger opponents outdistance his, when others are putting for eagle on the par fives and he's scrambling to get up and down for birdie? There is no way that a man with the pride of Mr. Nicklaus does not feel moments of sadness and regret in response to what he has lost along the way. But here lies the lesson to be learned. Examine how Jack Nicklaus deals with the process of aging and learn something about acceptance and adaptation, about loss and the willingness to compromise.

For the senior golfer, there exists today more than ever a wealth of technological aids to help your game persist in the face of declining physical prowess. Take advantage of oversized clubheads, graphite shafts, and shock-absorbing spongy grips. In the previous chapter, the importance of proper diet and exercise for all golfers was detailed. As a senior, it is more important than ever to keep your body limber and fueled with a nutritious food plan. If your distance off the tee is less than it used to be, make up for it on your second shot by learning to hit a fairway wood with consistent accuracy.

If you find yourself resisting suggestions such as these, you are probably struggling with ego-based issues that are also apparent in other areas of your life. Perhaps you insist that you can still perform heavy work, pushing yourself through it, refusing to admit that it might be too much for you. Maybe you refuse to wear a hearing aid, bifocals, or to take medication for high blood pressure. Or you just might avoid the issue of declining health entirely by refusing to go to the doctor for physical exams.

These are examples of denial, reflecting a refusal to acknowledge the reality of the aging process. Along with this denial comes the rejection of *solutions* to the problems of aging: ideas, philosophies, and technologies that can help life continue along more smoothly than you might imagine. If your eyesight has diminished and you love to read, there are large-print books and audio books. If you enjoyed jogging but your legs no longer permit it, there is always walking. If what you always loved most about golf was the big, booming drive, learn to appreciate the artistry of chipping one close. And if you find yourself thirsty with nothing but a couple of lemons in your possession, go ahead and make some lemonade. Or if you must, deny your plight and die from thirst.

It All Comes Down to Faith. If we stopped to examine life on this planet as we know it, we would have to admit that we don't really have a clue to what any of it means, or for that matter why we're here. Our minds have a way of protecting us from the horror of the "big picture." If we all spent our time obsessed with the reality that we exist on a microscopic rock that is spinning through the universe, there would be nobody left to supervise the psychiatric patients.

The developmental sequence of the life cycle protects us from the frightening realities about life and death. When young, most of us cannot conceptualize that we will someday die. We live our lives in an egocentric mode, believing that we are unique, that bad things are the stuff that gets written up in newspapers, is featured on the evening news, and happens to other people. As we advance into middle-age and senior years, we lose some of this irrational, albeit protective logic. It begins when we see our parents age and eventually die. Stepping into the "front row," we see the future with bone-chilling clarity.

As a man in his mid-forties who is fortunate enough to have both of his parents still alive and well, it's easy for me to suggest that seniors adapt to the aging process with acceptance and dignity. *I do realize that I will die someday.* But the voice that just wrote that sentence comes from a place that is hidden away somewhere, in a well-insulated corner of my psyche. I say I will die, but I don't think that I really believe it just yet. Senior golfers like Mort, who have the serenity and courage to live until they die, represent my ideal. Will I be out there joyfully playing nine when my every movement is strained, when my very best shot is more weak than powerful? I just don't know.

In the course of my professional experience I have had the good fortune to work with many individuals who were facing death and had the opportunity to learn a few things. I've observed the frightened, the angry, the bitter, and the depressed. And I've also witnessed those who felt ready to exit this life equipped with a sense of closure, gratitude, and peacefulness. The primary difference between the two varying perspectives seemed always to hinge upon the matter of faith . . . on the extent to which there was a belief in some form of a higher power, a belief that everything that happened in their lives—the good *and* the bad—happened exactly as it should have.

I don't know if the simple faith that enables aging gracefully is something that can be turned on like a light switch or for that matter can even be learned. Perhaps, like a solid golf swing, it is something that needs to be programmed into us at a very early age. But as is the case with a golf swing, it *can be* improved upon. The development of a sense of faith begins with the admission that it's something you want, and perhaps need. Because faith must invariably be blind, this is not an easy step for many to take. It's one thing to study a photograph of Ben Hogan's classic swing and allow it to serve as a theoretical ideal for your own eventual swing. It's not quite so easy to envision the face of God, and attempt to seek out the solace that comes to those who believe.

13

Putting It All Together

"The greatest breakthrough is taking your own sweet time to reach your goal, be it par or enlightenment."

—SHIVAS IRONS

I HAVE WRITTEN THIS BOOK THROUGH A WINTER AND INTO EARLY spring. It has been a mild winter, and the ground is unusually dry. The trees are budding, and the golf courses have opened up ahead of schedule. Friends have been calling, inviting me to come out and play, and until yesterday, I had resisted. I did not want to risk having a negative golf experience interfere with the completion of this book. I wanted to finish it feeling very much like the expert—confident in the validity of the theories I preach. But I know all too well that "plumbers have leaky pipes," and so I must confess to being a little bit afraid.

It was a cloudy and windy day with the temperature in the upper 40s. The course was surprisingly crowded considering the chilly conditions. When it was over, I rated it as "nine holes from hell." Feeling guilty for playing hooky from the word processor, feeling beaten by the strong winds, and feeling down about my array of pop-ups and grounders off the tee, I left the course determined to write the round off as an aberration. I went so far as to commit to forgetting it, to pretending that it never happened at all.

My denial scheme worked for about twenty-four hours. Then

it came back to me. Every moment, every detail. My friend and I were hooked up with a young big-hitter named Doug, and Charlie, an affable senior. During the first few holes, Charlie was my compatriot as he and I both struggled in contrast to the steady, powerful games of my friend and Doug. But after a few holes, Charlie's game also started to click. I, for the life of me, could not drive one down the middle of the fairway.

When you're struggling, it's the little things that can be especially annoying. Charlie, who was as nice a guy as you could hope to hook up with, had the habit of saying whenever he hit a good shot, "Even a blind chicken finds a piece of corn every now and then." The first time he said it, it was funny, cute, even endearing. However, after he parred 4, 5, and 6, enough was enough. I felt like taking my putter and wrapping it around his neck. He was dancing around the golf course, laughing and blaring out his "blind chicken" comment after every solid shot. I was bobbing my head, coming off the ball, and coming up empty. For this "blind chicken," there were no crushed drives, not a whole lot of laughter, and not a single piece of corn to be found.

I can laugh about it all now. I've been to the range and hit a few straight, and realize that before I know it, I'll again find the correct combination of fundamental elements in my swing that permit the ball to fly true to the target. And then I'll lose it for a while, get it back, lose it again, struggle with Hazards Three and Five, overcome them, and settle into a brief hot streak. This cyclical pattern will repeat itself until it's time to put away the clubs and spend the winter months fantasizing next season's new and improved swing, renewed work ethic, and better developed mental skills. And I'm not complaining. I love this process. It's not like I'm stuck on a treadmill, not making any progress. Each year I get a little bit closer to understanding my demons and knowing the feel of a proper golf swing. It's just that life is an ongoing process that requires a whole lot of patience, and golf is a whole lot like life.

This book or any book about the ongoing process of life and/ or golf cannot conclusively end. There will always be more to say and even more to learn. But end it I must, and until the time comes for the sequel, the following sections will have to suffice as the wrap-up to *Golf's Mental Hazards*. My hope is that you will make good use of what you have learned about *your* mental hazards at this particular moment in *your* life and, as a result, that your ability to perform effectively on the golf course, as well as in the course of your everyday life, will have evolved accordingly.

Fun's Still the Bottom Line

THROUGHOUT THIS BOOK, I HAVE EQUATED THE CHALLENGE OF golf improvement with issues of life and death intensity. This may not have helped the average golfer to lighten up and simply enjoy the game. It's easy for recreational golfers to forget that *golf is just a game* played primarily for the purpose of escaping, unwinding, and having fun. To forget that even though golf has the power to elicit the full gamut of emotions, and even though you can learn about yourself and grow as a person from your experience as a golfer, it still remains a game. A game that is meant to be fun. When golf performance becomes confused with issues of self-worth and identity, the stakes escalate to the point where it is no longer a game. Rather it has become an excuse, a method for avoiding as opposed to solving "real-life" problems.

Even professional golfers—whose livelihood and identity *do* depend to a great extent on golf performance—are not so foolish as to tie too much of themselves to their games. In the early part of the 1995 season, Peter Jacobsen went on a tear, winning the AT & T Pebble Beach Pro-Am and the Buick Invitational on consecutive weeks. During an interview that was broadcast during the third round of The Players Championship, Jacobsen was asked if he had gotten more serious, more intense about his game. He replied, "I'm probably less serious about my game than I was in the past. I've lost a brother and a father in the past six years. And what about people who have lost friends and comrades in wars? Golf is a game. You've got to keep that in perspective."

While Paul Azinger had to leave the Tour in order to receive treatment for cancer, he had a firsthand lesson in the kind of perspective that Peter Jacobsen talked about. During his absence, he was quoted as saying, "I feel as secure and content and happy as I have ever felt in my life. As bad as the treatments were, it has been a wonderful six months home with my wife and kids. It's been a great time off the course to reflect on where my happiness really comes from."

Listening to the words of these great golfers, don't you feel just a little ashamed? Think about how disappointed you become when your play doesn't meet your expectations. Is this kind of reaction really necessary? Considering that I'm not one to talk, I'm going to talk just the same. I know that sometimes it's not easy to simply have fun playing the game. I know that golf has a way of bringing out the dark moods in even the most positively spirited of individuals. As ridiculous as it may sound, one of the greatest challenges presented by golf may be to learn how to have fun with it. I'm not just talking about looking forward to playing, or dreaming about great moments from yesterday's or tomorrow's round. I'm referring to going out and having fun, of playing as if you were a kid again. Kids know how to have fun, and they have lots of it when they are playing their favorite games.

When I coached my son's Little League squad of 7- and 8-year-olds, I marveled at the pure joy I observed in the faces of those kids. It was the parents who brought everyone down. I recall the kid who stood in the batter's box as his father stood behind the cage and yelled out instructions such as "Stay back on the pitch," "Don't step in the bucket," "Keep the bat high," "Take a good rip at it." When the poor, overwhelmed child finally struck out, the father would shake his head and inform his son that "We'll get 'em next time. We've got to practice more. That's all." As soon as the kid escaped his old man's scrutiny and got back to his peers in the dugout, it was back to laughing and horseplay. Winning was clearly not the most important thing. It was running to cash in chips for an ice pop when the game was over. At 7 years of age, it just didn't matter that much. Having fun was the name of the game.

It might be impossible for an adult to think and feel with the unrestricted innocence of a child, but there is a lesson to be learned from the kids. Watch them experience the unpolluted joy of fresh air and movement, alive in the moment, unrestricted by fear, ego-needs, and self-consciousness. Then think about the quality of your own experiences on the golf course. Most likely, you experience more joy, approach the game more like a child, when you are playing well. But unfortunately, if you're like everyone else in the world, every day quite simply cannot be a good day. And if you're like every golfer who ever played the game, there will be a substantial number of days when you will be disappointed with your performance, knowing you could have done better.

On the down days, remember to ask yourself how much a flubbed drive or a missed putt would matter if you lost your job or if someone you loved was seriously ill. I'm not suggesting you become so lax as to not care about your performance, but know where to draw the line. Learn to go out there and bear down, give it all you have if it suits you. Embrace your shining moments, rejoice in them, lap them up for all they're worth. But on those days when it's not to be, make a concerted effort to think like a kid, to let go of the intensity and find a little joy. On days such as these, go so far as to consider the advice of Shivas Irons who said that "one must know when to quit, and even when to collapse . . . There is a time for lettin' the bottom drop out, for forgettin' yer score entirely, for forgettin' yer mental tricks and devices, for just swingin' any ol' way ye please." After all, who's better off? The 15-handicapper who shot an 83 and can't stop thinking about the missed opportunities to break 80 or the 25-handicapper who shot a 108 and had the time of his life? If fun is not the bottom line when you tee it up, you need to carefully reconsider the benefit of teeing it up at all.

Self-Acceptance and the Problem of Perfectionism

MOST PEOPLE WANT TO BE SOMEONE THEY'RE NOT. THE DRAMATIC actor wants to do comedy, Michael Jordan wants to play baseball, and the steady but short 20-handicapper wants to reach par fives in two. Nervous people want to be calmer, passive people want to be more assertive, and gregarious people would like to sit back and be able to listen more effectively. Most people are always looking outside of themselves, at how others behave and at what others have, and in the process, fail to notice the treasures buried in their own backyard.

Even if the grass does always appear greener on the other side of the dogleg-left, as a mature adult you have hopefully come to realize that nothing in life is perfect. Not love, not work, not people, not the way you look, the way you feel, or the way you swing a golf club. If you have managed to recover from the disappointment of this realization—and many people never do —you are in a position to adapt accordingly and begin the process of self-exploration, self-improvement, and ultimately self-acceptance.

The basic objective of this book has been to provide you with a blueprint for embarking on the journey through this process of growth—for overcoming Golf's Mental Hazards and for putting an end to the self-destructive round. During the course of this journey, you have learned that the very qualities that sabotage golf performance may also impact negatively in other areas of your life, that to be a better golfer requires that you also be a better person, or vice versa. The program began with the development of insight through the administration of the *MHAS*. Next, came the presentation of techniques specifically tailored to overcoming each of the six of Golf's Mental Hazards. If you have taken my suggestions seriously, and continue to practice them with patience and diligence, there will definitely be positive growth in your golf game and in your personal life as well. But no matter how much you invest yourself in the pursuit of change, there will remain a piece of your basic self that will live on, that cannot change.

When a golf pro handed me a 7-iron for the first time five years ago, it was the start of a new life. I was excited, filled with hope, had no idea how good I could be if I put my mind to it. I discovered that with hard work, I could improve steadily, and develop a respectable game. But there were limits. No matter how much I turned my shoulders and worked on the fundamentals of proper weight shift, the physics of my anatomy would not permit the 250-yard drive. I recall the unpleasantness of outdoing myself and hitting it 220 in the fairway, and still being the shortest off the tee. Just a couple of years into the game, and I felt bad about a decent poke down the middle.

I once heard a saying that it's sometimes a good idea to place the yardstick behind you instead of in front of you. To take a look at all you've already accomplished instead of worrying about what lies ahead, the work that still "needs" to be done. I have done my very best to follow this advice. I can't say that I've succeeded in always feeling good about all parts of my game, but I do know that I have gotten to a point where I accept it for what it is. I know my limits and strengths and have learned to play within myself

As compensation for not being particularly long off the tee, I have worked hard at and developed a terrific, compensatory wedge game. I've experienced the joy of frustrating big hitters with a relentless and pesky style of play ("You're only lying three?"), and of playing smart enough to take money from "better" golfers than myself. Am I satisfied with my progress as a golfer? Sometimes yes and sometimes no. On bad days, I'd give up ten strokes to be able to consider cutting a dogleg, or to think about reaching a par five in two. On good days, I feel devilishly smart when I take the bunkers out of play by laying up on my second shot to a long, tough par four. I'm pitching up to make bogey at worst, while my more adept partners very well might be taking two out of a trap for a spirit-breaking six. On good days, I like my game and I like who I am.

There's a good deal about yourself that you can understand and change, along with a good part that simply needs to be accepted. If you continue to look at others, wanting to be someone you're not, you will never be satisfied with any aspect of your life, and your self-esteem will continue to suffer. If you're smart, you'll know your strengths and compensate for your weaknesses. You will remain busy at the work of changing the things that are in your power to change, and you will have the realistic expectation of making *progress* and not expecting *perfection*. Follow this plan faithfully, and you will see vast progress in your golf game as well as in the general quality of your life. Accepting all the things about yourself that you wish were different but are powerless to change, learning to take pride in "playing your game," is the final step to serenity, peace of mind, and a lower handicap.

Now That All Your Dreams Have Come True

LET'S SAY THAT YOU'RE NOT THE GREATEST GOLFER, BUT YOU HAVE a steady game that you feel good about. You have read this book carefully and feel that you have learned a good deal about overcoming Golf's Mental Hazards to the point where you rarely self-destruct during a round. Let's also say that you have a solid family, some good friends, enjoy your job, and even feel satisfied with the money you make (okay, I'll concede that this last one might be impossible). Now that you've reached a point in your life where all is going well—when all your dreams have finally come true—you have finally earned the right to simply sit back, relax, and enjoy the ride.

Wake up! Time to get real. There are bills to be paid, the basement is wet, your boss is a control freak who likes to play head games, and your golf performance is about as erratic as your teenager's temperament. If these concerns don't apply, fill in the blanks with the details that portray your particular set of problems. This is life. Solve one problem and up springs another. It's a lot like closet space. You grow into whatever you have and always find yourself in need of a little bit more.

Nowhere is the pattern of chronic dissatisfaction more clearly demonstrated than in the game of golf. And perhaps herein lies one of the great lures of this great game—the fact that it can never be mastered. Pitchers can throw a perfect game and bowlers can roll a 300, but a golfer will never shoot an 18. Like the carrot dangled in front of the donkey, the game will continue to taunt and tease and nudge the golfer along. No matter how good a golfer you become, it will *never* be enough. And even if all of your other dreams *do* somehow manage to come true, you can always count on golf to keep you going in the direction of perfection and impossibility.

During his address at the dinner to kick off the USGA's Centennial celebration, John Updike had this to say on the subject: "When I was first asked to speak to you this evening, my first thought was 'Oh, no. My golf is not nearly good enough!' But then I reflected that one of the charms of the game is that nobody's golf, not even Fred Couples's and Nick Faldo's, is good enough to please them and their supporters all the time. Golf is a game that almost never fails, even at the highest levels on which it can be played, to mar a round with a lapse or two, and that at the other extreme rarely fails to grant even the most abject duffer, somewhere in his or her round, with a wayward miracle of a good shot."

The dissatisfaction inherent in golf finds its basis in human nature. For individuals, families, communities, and civilizations to move forward, there needs to be a certain degree of unresolved tension. A life of complete satisfaction is a complacent life, a stagnant life, a life that is not propelled by the mental anguish of conflict, indecision, and problem-solving. Like the spring in a wind-up toy car, the coiling and uncoiling of the golf swing, hunger, pain, or the desire to be respected, it is tension and dissatisfaction that generate the power to move forward. The fully realized life is a life without a future, a life without hope, a life that is over.

Golf is a wonderful setting to entertain and learn about frustration, conflict, resolution, and growth. It is the perfect laboratory to experiment with the mental hazards that keep tripping you up, that prevent you from realizing your dreams. Be it par or a new business venture, a bigger house or a smaller ego, you are simulating the work that needs to be done every time you stand over a golf ball and prepare to swing. So put your best stroke on it and don't get down when you shank one or pull it into the woods. There is always the next shot on which to recover. And the next one, and then the next one, and then the one after that. And if you find yourself in the midst of one of those days where it seems as if you'll never strike a golf ball solidly again, don't believe it. Hang in tough, head held high, secure in the knowledge that even a blind chicken finds a piece of corn every now and then.

APPENDIX

The Research Sample

THE *MHAS* was given to 270 golfers from various public and private golf clubs in the Northeast region as well as to golfers who attended golf school seminars that I had conducted. The accompanying table on page 218 summarizes these data. The sample was broken down and analyzed on the basis of the following three factors:

1. Sex. The average scores for the 187 males who participated in the research sample fell into the moderate range for all six mental hazards. This indicates that the average scores for *all* males was similar to the average scores for the entire research sample, which also included 83 females.

The female subgroup's average score for Hazard Two fell into the low range of the Mental Hazard Profile. This same subgroup's average score on Hazard Four was higher than the average score of the entire sample for this hazard, falling in the elevated range of the Mental Hazard Profile. In effect, this indicates that the females in the sample experience less difficulty with anger (Hazard Two) and more difficulty with self-consciousness (Hazard Four) than the males who were part of the research sample.

2. Age. The age range was divided into four groups: younger than 30 (55 subjects), 30–40 (70 subjects), 41–55 (90 subjects), and older than 55 (55 subjects). Note that this breakdown does not take the sex of the participants into account and therefore all four age groups consist of both males and females. For the six mental hazards, all four age groups yielded average scores that fell into the moderate range of the Mental Hazard Profile, with three exceptions. (1) The younger than 30 subgroup yielded an average score for Hazard Two that fell into the elevated range on the Mental Hazard Profile. (2) The older than 55 subgroup's average score for Hazard One fell into the elevated range. (3) The older than 55 subgroup's average score for Hazard Two was in the low range of the Mental Hazard Profile.

A summary of age-related results indicates that individuals in the research sample who were under 30, experience more difficulty with anger (Hazard Two) than the research sample as a whole. The subgroup that consisted of individuals who were older than 55 experienced more anxiety (Hazard One) and less anger (Hazard Two) than the entire research sample.

3. Handicap. The research sample was divided into three subgroups on the basis of handicap: 0–10 (63 subjects), 11–20 (88 subjects), and greater than 20 (119 subjects). This breakdown did not consider sex or age of the participants, so all three subgroups consist of males and females of varying ages. Average scores for the low-handicap (0–10) subgroup fell into the low range of the Mental Hazard Profile for four of the six mental hazards (Hazards One, Two, Three, and Six were low). Their average scores for Hazards Four and Five were in the moderate range. Middle-handicap golfers (11–20) yielded average scores that fell into the moderate range for all six hazards. High-handicappers (greater than 20) were moderate for Hazards One through Five, however, obtained an elevated subgroup average for Hazard Six.

In summary, low handicappers in the research sample experience less anxiety (Hazard One), less anger (Hazard Two), less moodiness (Hazard Three), and a better work ethic (Hazard Six) than the research sample as a whole. Middle- and high-handicappers' average subgroup scores were the same as the whole research sample with the exception of the high-handicapper's report of having a poorer work ethic (Hazard Six).

These findings are intended to help you put your own Mental Hazard Profile into a meaningful perspective. For instance, if you are an under-30-year-old male who scored in the elevated range for Hazard Two, it might help you to see that this problem is not uncommon for a young male. Conversely, if you are older than 55 and scored in the elevated range for Hazard Two, your behavior is less common and probably worthy of careful consideration.

AVERAGE SCORES FOR SUBGROUPS IN RESEARCH SAMPLE

HAZARD	ONE	TWO	THREE	FOUR	FIVE	SIX
SEX						
Males (187)	MOD	MOD	MOD	MOD	MOD	MOD
Females (83)	MOD	LOW	MOD	ELEV	MOD	MOD
AGE						
Under 30 (55)	MOD	ELEV	MOD	MOD	MOD	MOD
30-40 (70)	MOD	MOD	MOD	MOD	MOD	MOD
41-55 (90)	MOD	MOD	MOD	MOD	MOD	MOD
Over 55 (55)	ELEV	LOW	MOD	MOD	MOD	MOD
HANDICAP						
0-10 (63)	LOW	LOW	LOW	MOD	MOD	LOW
11-20 (88)	MOD	MOD	MOD	MOD	MOD	MOD
Over 20 (119)	MOD	MOD	MOD	MOD	MOD	ELEV

Numbers in parentheses indicate how many individuals from the research sample were included in the subgroup.

MENTAL HAZARD ASSESSMENT SCALE

RETEST RESPONSE SHEET

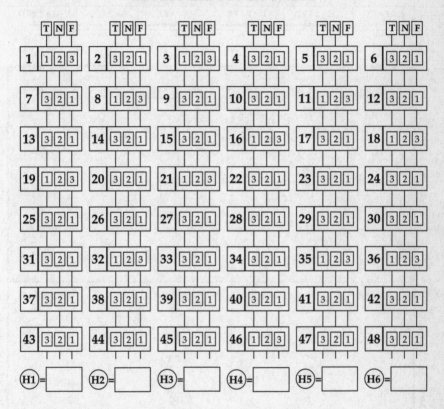

Calculate Your Scores

For each of the six columns, add up the eight numbers that are in the boxes that you have checked. Enter six totals in the boxes labeled H1 through H6. Your scores will range from eight to twenty-four.

Transfer Your Score to Your Mental Hazard Profile

Take each of the six scores for H1-H6 and enter them in the appropriate squares which are located across the top of the Mental Hazard Profile, found on the following page. Circle the number in the column which runs down from each of the six scores.

MENTAL HAZARD PROFILE

HAZARD ONE	HAZARD TWO	HAZARD THREE	HAZARD FOUR	HAZARD FIVE	HAZARD SIX
21-24	21-24	20-24	21-24	22-24	22-24
20	20	19	20	21	21
19	19	18	19	20	20
18	18	17	18	19	19
17	17	16	17	18	18
16	16	15	16	17	17
15	15	14	15	16	16
14	14	13	14	15	15
13	13	12	13	14	14
12	12	11	12	13	13
11	11	10	11	12	12
-	-	-	-	11	11
10	10	9	10	10	10
9	9	-	9	9	9
8	8	8	8	8	8

ELEVATED RANGE (rows 21-24 through 16)

MODERATE RANGE (rows 15 through 12)

LOW RANGE (rows 11 through 8)

REFERENCES AND SUGGESTED READINGS

Azinger, Paul, with Ken Abraham. *Zinger.* Grand Rapids (MI): Zandervan Publishing House, 1995.

Barrett, David. "A Zinger of a Comeback," New York: *Golf Magazine*, August, 1994, pp. 68–69.

Becker, Ernest. *The Denial of Death.* New York: Free Press, 1973.

Blanchard, Ken. *Playing the Great Game of Golf.* New York: William Morrow, 1992.

Boswell, Thomas. "It's All About Attitude," New York: *Golf Magazine*, February, 1995, pp. 23–24.

Brown, Robert A. *The Golfing Mind.* New York: Lyons & Burfield, 1994.

Brumer, Andy. "The Price Is Right," New York: *The Golfer*, 1995 Yearbook, pp. 36–42.

Burnett, Jim. "Learning to Be a Star," New York: *Golf Magazine*, January, 1995, pp. 54–55.

Burns, David D. *Feeling Good: The New Mood Therapy.* New York: Avon Books, 1980.

Charlesworth, Edward A., and Nathan, Ronald G. *Stress Management.* New York: Ballantine Books, 1982.

Cohn, Patrick J. *The Mental Game of Golf.* South Bend (IND): Diamond Communications, 1994.

Coop, Richard H., with Bill Fields. *Mind Over Golf.* New York: Macmillan, 1993.

Covey, Stephen R. *The 7 Habits of Highly Effective People.* New York: Simon & Schuster, 1989.

Dodson, James, "Archaeologist of the Soul," New York: *Golf Magazine*, March, 1995, pp. 23–30, 176.

Douillard, John. *Body, Mind and Sport.* New York: Crown Trade Paperbacks, 1994.

Dye, Peter, with Mark Shaw. *Bury Me in a Pot Bunker.* Reading (MA): Addison-Wesley, 1995.

Enhager, Kjell. *Quantum Golf: The Path to Golf Mastery.* New York: Warner Books, 1991.

Fasciana, Guy S. *Golf's Mental Magic.* Holbrook (MA): Bob Adams, 1992.

Frankl, Viktor, E. *Man's Search for Meaning.* New York: Washington Square Press, 1963.

Gallwey, W. Timothy. *The Inner Game of Golf.* New York: Random House, 1981.

Garfield, Charles A., with Hal Zina Bennett. *Peak Performance: Mental Training Techniques of the World's Greatest Athletes.* Los Angeles: Jeremy P. Tarcher, 1984.

Graham, David, with Guy Yocum. *Mental Toughness Training for Golf.* New York: Pelham Books, 1990.

Haultain, Arnold. *The Mystery of Golf.* Bedford (MA): Applewood Books (reissue), 1908.

Herrigel, Eugen. *Zen in the Art of Archery.* New York: Vintage Books, 1989.

Hogan, Ben. *Five Lessons: The Modern Fundamentals of Golf.* New York: Simon & Schuster, 1957.

Hogan, Chuck, with Dale Van Dalsem and Susan Davis. *Five Days to Golfing Excellence.* Sedona (AZ): T & C Publishing, 1986.

Jamison, Steve. "Making Golf Work," New York: *Golf Magazine,* October, 1994, pp. 72–73.

Jansen, Dan, with Mary Ellin Barrett. "Winning the Mind Game," Arlington (VA): *USA Weekend,* July 15–17, 1994, pp. 4–6.

Jenkins, Dan. *Fairways and Greens.* New York: Doubleday, 1994.

Jobe, Frank W., et al. *Exercise Guide to Better Golf.* Inglewood (CA): Champion Press, 1994.

John-Roger and McWilliams, Peter. *Do It! Let's Get Off Our Buts.* Los Angeles: Prelude Press, 1991.

Jonge, Peter de. "A Zone of His Own: Tiger Woods," New York: *The New York Times Magazine,* February 5, 1995, pp. 36–39.

King, Randy. "Sam Snead: Wishing He Could Turn Back Time," New York: *On Tour* (PGA Tour publication), January/February, 1995, pp. 11–13.

Lakein, A.L. *How to Get Control of Your Time and Your Life.* New York: Peter Wyden, 1973.

Links, Bo. *Follow the Wind.* New York: Simon & Schuster, 1995.

Loehr, James E. *The New Toughness Training for Sports.* New York: Dutton, 1994.

Mackenzie, Marlin M. *Golf the Mind Game.* New York: Dell, 1990.

Miller, Larry. *Holographic Golf.* New York: Harper Collins, 1993.

Mitchell, John. "Golf in the 'Hood," New York: *Golf Magazine*, February, 1993, pp. 112–116.

Moore, Charles W. "The Mental Hazards of Golf" (1929), in Thomas P. Stewart. *A Tribute to Golf*. Harbor Springs (MI): Stewart, Hunter and Assoc., 1990.

Moretti, Bill. "Take a Tip From the Other Side," New York: *Golf Magazine*, April, 1994, pp. 132–133.

Murphy, Michael. *Golf in the Kingdom*. New York: Dell, 1972.

Nakken, Craig. *The Addictive Personality*. San Francisco: Harper & Row, 1988.

Nicklaus, Jack, with Ken Bowden. *Golf My Way*. New York: Simon & Schuster, 1974.

Nicklaus, Jack, with Ken Bowden. "My Strongest Weapon," New York: *Golf Magazine*, December, 1993, pp. 44–49.

Nicklaus, Jack, with Ken Bowden. "Ageless Golf," New York: *Golf Magazine*, March, 1995, pp. 43–53.

Peck, M. Scott. *The Road Less Traveled*. New York: Simon & Schuster, 1978.

Penick, Harvey. *Harvey Penick's Little Red Book*. New York: Simon & Schuster, 1992.

Pirozzolo, Fran. "Mind Power," New York: *Golf Magazine*, December, 1994, p. 45.

Player, Gary. *Fit for Golf*. New York: Simon & Schuster, 1995.

Pressfield, Steven. *The Legend of Bagger Vance*. New York: William Morrow, 1995.

Rotella, Robert J., and Bunker, Linda K. *Mind Mastery for Winning Golf*. Englewood Cliffs (NJ): Prentice-Hall, 1981.

Rotella, Bob, with Bob Cullen. *Golf Is Not a Game of Perfect*. New York: Simon & Schuster, 1995.

Redfield, James. *The Celestine Prophecy*. New York: Warner, 1994.

Suzuki, Shunryu. *Zen Mind, Beginner's Mind*. New York: Weatherhill, 1970.

United States Golf Association (eds. Amy Janello and Brennon Jones). *Golf the Greatest Game*. New York: Harper Collins, 1994.

Updike, John. "John Updike on Golf" (transcription of USGA Centennial celebration speech), Far Hills (NJ): *Golf Journal*, March/April, 1995, pp. 6–7.

Van Kampen, Kenneth. *Visual Golf*. New York: Simon & Schuster, 1992.

Waggoner, Glen. *Divots, Shanks, Gimmes, Mulligans, and Chili Dips*. New York: Villard Books, 1993.

Wallach, Jeff. *Beyond the Fairway*. New York: Bantam Books, 1995.

Weathers, Ed. "Nerves," Trumbull (CT): *Golf Digest*, October, 1994, pp. 69–75.

Wheelis, Allen. *How People Change.* New York: Harper & Row, 1973.

Williams, Redford, and Williams, Virginia. *Anger Kills.* New York: HarperCollins, 1993.

Wind, Herbert Warren. *Following Through.* New York: Harper Perennial, 1985.

Wiren, Gary, and Coop, Richard. *The New Golf Mind.* New York: Simon & Schuster, 1978.

Wodehouse, P.G. *The Golf Omnibus.* New York: Wing Books, 1973.